THE CYNICAL BASTARD

A personal tirade by

DAVID GUDGEON

iUniverse, Inc.

New York   Bloomington

The Cynical Bastard

iUniverse books may be ordered through booksellers or by contacting:

iUniverse
1663 Liberty Drive
Bloomington, IN 47403
www.iuniverse.com
1-800-Authors (1-800-288-4677)

Because of the dynamic nature of the Internet, any Web addresses or links contained in this book may have changed since publication and may no longer be valid. The views expressed in this work are solely those of the author and do not necessarily reflect the views of the publisher, and the publisher hereby disclaims any responsibility for them.

ISBN: 978-1-4502-3470-2 (pbk)
ISBN: 978-1-4502-3471-9 (ebk)

Printed in the United States of America

iUniverse rev. date: 11/9/10

Contents

1. Preface 1

2. Things I Don't Like 3

3. Things People Have Not Learned 51

4. Things That Should Be Made Into Law 61

5. Legal vs. Illegal 68

6. What Is It With… 76

7. Whatever Happened To… 82

8. Pet Peeves 91

9. Wouldn't It Be Fun? 112

10. People Are 115

11. Phrases That I Hate 138

12. The Big Lie 150

13. The End Of An Empire 158

14. In Closing 161

Preface

Well, I'll just warn you right now. If you were looking for a feel-good book then you may as well put this down and run, do not walk to the nearest exit. When I wrote this, I was not in a good mood. I was angry at the world and I will make the whole world angry at me with what is put to paper here.

I do not base anything written here purely in fact, although some things may be fact or considered that way by the reader. I therefore do not provide anything to back up any claim made here. Really, this is what one would consider to be entirely opinion based, and I may not even really believe most of what I have to say myself. A lot of what I say here is a lot of what people think and are afraid to say, whether it is true or not and whether it can be proven or not. I am expressing my supposed right to free speech, a privilege that many Americans have become afraid to exercise in recent years. So for all intensive purposes we will just call the contents herein a lot of opinion and leave it at that.

Needless to say that the things described here do not necessarily pertain to everyone or anyone at any particular time, but the things described here pertain to enough people and often enough to have pissed me off enough to write them down.

I am sure that you will find much of it humorous up until you come across something that may pertain to you and then you are going to get upset. Well, tough… We all get upset and no amount of politically correct programming will change it or cover it up. It's your right to be upset sometimes, so get upset and quit worrying about what other people are going to think. I am not going to pretend to be nice to make anyone feel good about themselves, and no-one should have to.

So In other words, *"stop being a weenie"*.

Things I Don't Like

I am a big jerk, and there are a lot of things I don't like. But I find that I am not the only one who doesn't like them, I am just one of the rare few who is not afraid to publically admit that I don't like them. Most people are too afraid of criticism and reproach to speak their minds. I am not afraid. I will say whatever the hell I want. If someone doesn't like it, they don't have to listen. And as much of a prick I am about my opinions, I am not offended by other people's opinions. They can believe whatever they want as well. I am also not intimidated by being wrong. I can be wrong. It's okay if I am. That is how one learns. Although I admit that I am rather hardheaded, and telling me I am wrong is no easier than telling anyone else, but at least I can accept someone not believing what I do.

Clearance Sales

It is amazing what some people are willing to do in order to take advantage of a discount. And of course I am not talking about shopping the circulars and clipping coupons. That is no big deal. I am talking about stampeding people trampling their fellow man to save some change. One has to imagine the extremes that people will lower themselves to for the sake of a few dollars. And honestly, it's not that hard to imagine.

Often, we hear about sales where people are literally trampled, sometimes to death at grand openings or day after Thanksgiving sales, (it's not called black Friday for nothing)! This is the human condition at its most exposed form. The true baseness of humanity on display like raw nerves in a tooth with all the selfishness, ruthlessness and violence people can muster at its Sunday best. Forget about bigotry, rape, murder and child abuse, if you truly want to see the evil of people, put something desirable on sale with a limited supply, open the doors and roll the film.

People also tend to be very stupid about certain items that are on sale. I would have to think that just about every base nitwit in the Western world must understand at this point that electronics are virtually worthless, and lose their value daily as new items are enhanced and upgraded. You see this with cell phones all the time. You no sooner get it activated and the new model is out and making your phone obsolete. Video games are even worse. You trample children and the elderly at four in the morning at a department store because only fifty of some new model is offered around the holiday, only to have it available for less than half price a few months later when demand is down. How stupid is that?

Well, here is how it works nitwits. The initial high price is so that the company can recover its investment into the development and manufacture of the item. As this is recovered, the price goes down and is put on sale and eventually clearanced out in order to make room for the upgrade model that is moving along next. This is done to get your money because you are dumb enough to get sucked into this trap. The technology is there, and is being held back deliberately so that every possible dime can be milked out of the consumer public. Are you going to tell me that a personal desktop computer can only manage say 8 to 12 gigs of ram, but you can get a portable storage that fits in your wallet that holds 64 gigs? You can't tell me that you don't see something out of balance here.

The reality is that people know they are being hosed, and they allow it to happen. The technology is there, but you will never see the true breadth of its wonder in your lifetime.

Free

Try this free, buy one get one free, free trial, free service free sample, free gift, free toy, free accommodations, free shit and free lies. I hate this word, free. Free is a seriously abused word in the English language, and it should be restrained. There is nothing wrong with the word itself; it is the usage I have a problem with. Everybody offers something for nothing, which is a lie because there is a string attached to everything, and then personifies it with the word free.

Surely people must realize that if you have to buy one thing to get the other, then the other is not free, it has been acquired by condition. You are not buying one thing to get another free; you are buying two and getting half off. No-one is actually giving you anything. Who believes this shit? I mean really, you can't even die for free. Everything costs someone something somewhere and somehow. We all pay.

Freedom

Freedom is even worse. From this perspective, nobody is really free. The only way you can be truly free in this sense is if you were living in your own mind, and then you are still your own prisoner. So who is free? Not people. And I don't want to hear about hermits or monks either. If they were really free they wouldn't live hidden away from society, if they are in hiding, they are not free. These people are in a self imposed solitary confinement against the social order, this is not freedom. This is fear.

Pacifists

In a nutshell, a pacifist is someone who never had to defend their own life. A pacifist is also someone who never had to defend the life of a loved one. Rarely ever, will you see a human animal literally stand idly by and allow themselves to be murdered, or allow someone they truly care about to be murdered simply because they refuse to fight on account of some moral implication. If a person stands down in a life or death situation, it is rarely ever by way of pacifism, it is more likely by way of fear. That is not pacifism, that is cowardice.

Stereotypes

Stereotypes are destructive and useless, and very often self imposed. People believe what they believe because they think they are supposed to believe it, not because it is true and not because they believe it to be true. A fantastic example of this is in the areas of fashion and music. Both are pop culture subjects, and both are highly stereotyped. Fashion and music are deliberately aimed at specific groups of people who sheepishly eat it up because they believe that they are supposed to. Not because they like it and not because it is right for them or because of culture, but because they think that is what they are supposed to like and what they are supposed to do. Stereotypes asphyxiate creative thought and individualism. Why can't a Chinese guy be a great hockey player and a black guy be a great ballet dancer? Why is it that you don't see an Eskimo gospel singer? Because they have convinced themselves that they are not supposed to do these things. They have stereotyped themselves. Self stereotyping is a weakness.

Vampires

I don't know about the rest of you, but I have had it up to the eyeballs with the whole retarded cute teen vampire bullshit. There is nothing cute or cuddly about a bacteriologically enhanced human who becomes a predator of other humans. This person is in effect a sort of cannibal if they feed on human blood. The media targets young people with this trash deliberately because they suck it up, (pun intended). Then you end up with all these wasteland teenagers who pretend they are vampires so much they start believing it because their self esteem is so pathetically low. I am sick of teenage vampire books and movies. Give it a rest. Vampires suck...

Charity

Now, I'm not knocking every charity here. Some are helpful and some are useful and some mean well, but there is a limit where my tolerance is concerned. I am so sick and tired of all these charities that are constantly crawling and sniveling and begging from every possible direction and from every possible medium day in and day out. Enough already!

Leave me the fuck alone! If I wanted to give something, I would do it. Stop groveling for my spare change.

The problem here is that people have become so accustomed to it that they will give a donation, even a small one, just to get some peace and quiet from the charity beggar and make them go away. But instead of this being the occasional thing it has become the norm and now we are subjected to nonstop harassment from charity organizations begging from dusk till dawn every day of our lives. This is too much. You can't save everybody and you shouldn't try. And this is not the true purpose of charity to begin with. You will never save the world from its problems by throwing money at it. When you do nothing but throw money at a problem what you often end up doing is enabling the problem instead. Stop being an enabler!

Humans are inherently lazy. If you teach them that they can hustle their way through the system, they will. If you really want to help, get involved for real so that you know where your money and efforts are going, don't just write a check and pat yourself on the back. Charity is a business, it makes money, your money.

Adult Entertainment

Okay, people like sex, I get it. I like sex. I enjoy it quite a bit in-fact. And I understand the idea behind voyeurism and I understand the idea behind watching porn to get a few kinky ideas to experiment with. Really, I do. But honestly, has anyone actually sat and watched this shit and really thought about it? Because seriously, it's pretty fucking stupid.

The plots are, well, there are no plots. And the acting is, well, there is nothing that can be constituted as acting. And the writing, um, is there any writing involved? Never mind the fact that a lot of it is degrading and humiliation based, that part is far too obvious. If your every fantasy is to treat a woman like a pile of shit, then pornography is for you.

But seriously, as far as my personal peeve, the thing that really pisses me off, (would you like to know what it is about porn that irritates me the most)? It's when this couple, or this threesome, say two girls and a guy, (which is how it should be, never with two guys) comes to an end and everybody stops what they are doing so the guy can jerk himself off to a finish. I hate that! What was the point? Why do all that work so you can whack yourself off? And the girl lays there and fakes an orgasm, (even though no-one is touching her, not even herself) and the guy is like "oh yeah, shit" and masturbates. And she's like, "yeah baby, give it to me, ohh". That is so fucking lame. That is so lame it makes me sick. I won't watch the shit. Besides, I would rather do it than watch it, (and no masturbation). They do all that jerking off shit because they know you are sitting in-front of the TV or the computer whacking off all by yourself and it helps you pretend that it's you. Ain't that nice of them? This is an industry based on entertaining the lonely, and that's pathetic.

Masturbation

While we are on the subject, I'm no big fan of masturbation either. Masturbation is a hobby typically of the lonely. There are some situations when you may do this when you are with another person as part of foreplay or some such thing, or mutual masturbation, (doing it to each other) I understand. But doing it all by yourself all the time is just sad. It's like, adult imaginary friend time. And despite what thousands of therapists will tell you, I think there is some detriment to it.

It goes like this. You are likely masturbating because you are not getting sex, or not getting enough, or not getting it the way that you need it, so you pretend to do it instead. But most likely you are doing it because you are not getting it at all, which means that you are lonely. And if you are pretending a function that is supposed to be both a healthy human recreation and a physical expression of intimacy, well, that is just depressing. I figured that out in my post-pubescent years. I used to feel depressed after, so the connection seemed obvious. Maybe it's just me, but I felt a lot better when I got away from masturbation and found the real thing!

Racism/Bigotry

This one couldn't be easier. Racists are stupid. People who orchestrate racists are not, because they collect dues and club fees and donations, and because they get to be popular, (even if it is just in the company of bigots).

Racist groups target knuckleheads deliberately because people who have learned not to think for themselves are easier to manipulate. People are lazy and like to be told what to do. Plus, when you are poorly educated you intimidate yourself out of rational thought because you feel less intelligent. Because you feel less intelligent, you feel less capable, and therefore you are less capable because you have told yourself that you are. The mind is the master, and will cripple you as well as help you when not disciplined, (keeping in mind that a disciplined mind need not be educated to be effective, poor education alone is not an excuse for being week willed against your own impulses). In keeping with the human condition, no-one wants to blame themselves for their own folly, so in order to preserve alleged dignity, someone else must be blamed. This is the easy part.

Why? You may ask; because the world provides a vast variety of color, religious and social selections to choose from. Pick a religion or a color you don't like, and blame them, it's their fault you are dumb. See, easy!

People are stupid in groups, but they are capable of great intelligence and understanding individually. So, assuming that I have an individual reading, then read carefully, and understand. Understand that when it comes to homo-sapiens, there is only one race, the human race. We are all the same species. All people of any type or color are all hybrids of an original type of person that no longer exists. We do not know for sure where this person came from originally, nor do we know for sure what he may have looked like, and honestly, it shouldn't matter. This person is the *proto-human* if you will. The same as all dogs are hybrids of the original type of dog, presumably the wolf. You can mix up any two dogs any which way, but you cannot breed a dog and a giraffe, because they are different species. If we were not all of one race by this understanding, we would not be compatible with other nationalities. That is why a person from Peru can have sex with a person from Scotland and produce a child. We are all a single species and came from the same stock. Physical differences between different people are a result of environmental elements that our ancestors were exposed to depending upon what region of the world they developed in. Darker people came from climates with intense sunlight, lighter people came from climates that were cold or had drastic seasonally changing climates, short stocky people came from mountainous regions, and so on.

So what's the difference? There really isn't one. The only true differences between people are social ones, religion, nationality, culture, language and of course, attitude. Not race. Since the differences are sociological ones, they are differences in our minds, and we can change our minds.

So stop looking for someone to blame for your troubles. Odds are, you need look no further than a mirror. Racism is a business. Understand this and you will understand racism in America.

Television

God, how I hate the television! What a horrible invention! Not from a technical perspective mind you. I mean, I get the point, cheap entertainment for the masses, really, I get it. But it has evolved out of control and become a monster. We have become enslaved to it. We sit there and watch other people's fake lives while we neglect living our own. We neglect our children, and use the TV as a babysitter so we don't have to be bothered with them. We use it as an excuse not to function in the real world while we waste away in a pretend world that exhibits little imagination and almost no education.

We have gone from three or four basic stations to literally hundreds of stations, and still can find nothing to watch. We sit there flipping stations constantly because we have learned to let our attention spans wander away, getting almost instantly bored because of the instant gratification at our disposal that is not gratifying in the least.

For those of you who are a little older, do not many of you think that the old programming from your youth was better? Ever wonder why? It is because with only a handful of stations only the most interesting of shows stood a chance, even if they were stupid shows. But now with cable and satellite cramming thousands of shows on hundreds of channels down your throat night and day these networks have to clamor for programs to fill the void. They will air any shit to fill the airspace and keep the network up and running, no matter how badly it's written or put together.

And please don't tell me about educational children's television. I grew up with this when it first came out, and it is not the same thing. The new shows are scrambling for children's attention at the same pace that the adult programming is, and shows no mercy in the process. I have the old shows on disc, and they are calm and peaceful and educational and entertaining in a way that people today can't understand anymore. The new shows are loud, aggressive, lack imagination and are geared in with advertising. These people are not trying to educate so much as sell something. And it is no substitution for human interaction, particularly with a young developing mind that needs and craves human attention for proper development. For Gods sakes, animals treat their young with more intimacy and compassion than many human parents currently do. Shut that fucking shit off and spend some time with your child before it turns into another you!

Someday aliens are going to fly by and pick up on our television transmissions and you know what will happen? They will euphonize this mudball because they will think it's a penal colony for the insane and decide to put us out of our misery. And you will have facilitated this by succumbing to watching trash on TV!

Telephones

Since we are in the electronics section, I may as well point out that I do not like telephones either. They are a great convenience, but they are a very abused tool. The idea behind the invention was for the expedience of information, nothing wrong with that. But the telephone can be used as a socially dysfunctional crutch as much as a tool for conveying information.

Look at it like this. When you are on your phone, you are not actually talking to anyone. You are talking to a machine that sends a signal to another machine that sends a signal to another machine that reconstructs that signal to sound like your voice so that the other person can hear it. It is not a real voice; it is not real social interaction. It is a transmission of communication, a tool of communication, and little else.

People know this, and don't realize that they do. Watch people on the phone. They will say things that they would never say and in a way that they would never say it, because they subconsciously know that they are talking to a little box instead of a person. Talking through a machine makes it impersonal, so ultimately no regard of the other listeners feelings are necessary. It is an over-convenience and an over-indulgence that is much abused.

Besides, no matter how many different features they add to cell-phones, (micro keyboards, cameras, digital recording, music library, etc) it is never what you really want. What I hear people ask for the most is longer battery life, better signal, higher durability, and waterproofing, (you know, that thing the insurance never seems to cover). I mean hell, if they can waterproof a digital camera, why not a cell-phone? Because then you don't have to keep buying new ones, that's why!

The Internet

The World Wide Web, the Information Super Highway our great modern internet. Cute Idea, been around longer than most people would know; made public only recently by comparison although you would think it has been here forever. But the truth is that it has not really been available on the scale by which it now exists for very long at all. And it certainly does not seem to be going in the direction that it was expected to.

The idea of linking people on a global scale for the purpose of communication and sharing information and knowledge is noble. It was a good idea, I admit it. But it has grown, and its growth has become perverse.

It would be easier to call the modern internet the pornography, advertising and celebrity gossip super highway as opposed to the Information Super Highway. The internet is loaded with trash, and is far too big to clean up. There is no way to accurately control it anymore. It cannot be policed. Now, I've got nothing against free speech, but I have watched the internet go from a virtual library to a virtual magazine stand practically overnight. It's a reflection of humanity and it's just embarrassing.

Machines

Let's just cut to the chase with all of this, I really just don't like machines period. It has nothing to do with the machinery itself, a lot of it is rather innovative and fascinating. There are a lot of useful electronic items out there that could really add to the human experience. And that is what they are supposed to do, add to the human experience. The problem comes from the human equation of the human experience. And that is, when you add humans to something, you fuck it up.

People use modern innovation as a crutch. It gives too many of them the opportunity to be lazy, and that is what I do not like. It also provides excuses not to interact with other people. Or to cut them out of a job so you can save like .12 an hour in wages.

Overpopulation

All anyone has to do is look around anymore to figure out that there are too damn many of us. People and the Earth are like mold on an orange; it keeps on spreading and getting worse by the day. There are so many damn people that nothing should be surprising anymore. Any weird shit you see in the news should not even raise the eyebrow of the average person anymore because with so many people nothing is impossible. Nothing surprises me now, no matter how bizarre or gruesome it is. I'm just like, "yeah, I could see that happening". How sad is that?

Never mind how badly we deplete resources, how much we displace other species and how much of a fucking mess we make in the process. We pretty much ruin everything we come in contact with, and keep on going without looking back. It's horrible, and we know it is and we keep right on doing it.

We hear scientists warning about diseases and plagues and how many tens of millions of people could be wiped out in some pandemic or another, but honestly now, if say

25 million people were to die suddenly of some new strain of flu tomorrow, would anyone really notice? That is like less than one half of one percent of the total population. That is like less than .50 cents out of a hundred dollar bill. And those numbers would be made back up by the end of the year at the rate that we breed.

Then people are told to use safe sex practices to control the population, (generally in severe poverty areas) and then warn that these practices do not always work. Then they want abstinence, and they ask for it from people who have such misery and poverty in their lives that sex is their only relief aside from death, and then wonder why they keep fucking, even with the threat of serious health risks and even death by way of sexually transmitted diseases. A warning from the W.H.O. is not going to stop them; they have nothing to lose anyway.

These people know it will kill them, and that is probably why they do it.

Mega Corporations

And by mega corporations, I mean these places that have like 5000 outlets nationwide, or 10,000 restaurants in like 50 countries, or branch offices all over the world. Mostly places like this are associated with mass production of consumer goods or with fast food, (which in a way is the same thing).

They overproduce unwanted and unneeded items by the millions in scales that are unimaginable to the average person, burning up resources on a global scale to produce badly manufactured unhealthy and unsafe items as cheaply as possible in order to turn a large profit by volume of sale.

They do not care about you. They don't. No matter what they say in any campaign or advertisement, they don't care. They only care about getting your money. And you will give it to them. You will give it to them because you do not understand the difference between quality and quantity. They know you don't understand the difference, and this is key to how they generate profit.

They also do not care about the environment. They have been raping the Earth and fouling it from day one, and know exactly what they are doing. They pretend to care for two main reasons. One, because pollution pisses a lot of people off and they don't want the bad press. And two, because there are a lot of government incentives to make nice with the environment, and that means more profit.

Advertising

I do not like advertising in any form. I mean, there is a valid point to it, that being to present an item or a service to be considered for sale. But the way in which it goes about treats people like they are completely stupid, and unfortunately, they are right. People are stupid and many of them can be easily convinced to buy into anything with very little effort.

Perhaps that is what troubles me about it. The fact that it is not so much how retarded the commercials are, but that people go for it. If people felt that their intelligence was being challenged, (which it is) with bad advertising then they would protest by not purchasing the product, or even writing the companies to complain. But they do not. They sit there flipping channels and drooling on their shirts while slowly being brainwashed into thinking that they need whatever shit is being presented. Haven't we wasted enough money and piled up enough junk? When does it end?

And what is with magazines? It's to the point where nearly half of a magazine is advertising. I have actually gotten lost flipping a magazine at the newsstand because I can't figure out what page some article or another is located due to the massive amount of printed ads. And what's worse, many of these articles turn out to be the ads! Enough!

Billboards have gotten worse as well. Now they have these new electronic billboards popping up all over the country. This is a form of advertisement based on the concept of everyone being programmed to stare at a screen. You watch TV all day and when you are not watching TV you are watching a monitor. This is just a giant monitor, and possibly a giant distraction, perhaps even the last distraction in some cases. Just think, a giant lighted TV screen flashing you casino and vodka advertisements on the highway at three in the morning while a semi pulling a trailer loaded with cows' cuts you off. What a way to die…

Social Services

And by social services, I mean organizations like child welfare. Now, I understand that in many cases this sort of intervention is absolutely necessary. There are a lot of kids out there being abused and often literally tortured by stupid and demented parents who are carrying on a cycle of violence that they were too weak to break themselves. I know, because I was one of these kids. Frankly, I'm lucky to be alive. And do you know what social services did for me? Nothing. Absolutely fucking nothing.

And additionally, I have worked with many children and watched social services sit back and watch abuse and still do nothing, even in the era from which this book has been written. This including my own kids, who the court finally took custody from the abusive parent, but then granted visitation so that they could continue to be manipulated by remote control.

I have witnessed this passing of the buck due to a lack of interest of any organization willing to make a move simply because they are waiting for another affiliated group to make a decision, so that they do not have to be the ones to do it. I suppose they are afraid of some legal action if they turn out to be wrong. As an example, you could say that the police do nothing because welfare has the kids and welfare does nothing because they are waiting on a court investigator who also does nothing because of an intervention group that has been brought on who also does nothing because their authority is superseded by child welfare. So nothing gets done, (at least not the right way).

It's like a basketball game where all these organizations are the players and your kid is the ball. It's three seconds to the buzzer an no-one is willing to even attempt taking a shot because they don't want to be the one who misses at the buzzer. Meanwhile, your kid is bounced all over the place and who wins? The other team wins. The child molester gets to go on molesting, or the tormenter goes right on tormenting and so on and so on because nobody wants responsibility.

Then there is the other extreme when some social worker gets in your business, decides they don't like you and you are either ruined or lose your kid over something foolish, and yet you are powerless to do anything about it because you are going up against the state government.

This is clearly a system that does not work, or at least does not work properly. But once again people, guess what? It is your fault that it doesn't work. People are no better with the responsibility factor than social services because people shirking their responsibility to their children in the first place have put the welfare department in charge of determining the fates of your families. And people being too weak willed to fight back, keeps them in that power.

Public Welfare

Ooh, you just knew this was next. Public welfare, the great beast itself! Where to even begin… The idea was a good one, you know; help people get back on their feet when they are down. Someone is out of work, someone is very young and pregnant and the father took off or the family disowns them. Good idea turned really bad.

Nowadays, the welfare system does one of two things. It acts as an enabler, or it cripples you. It acts as an enabler because lazy or corrupted people will abuse the system deliberately. These types of people are always looking for a shortcut, and often by way of a handout through hustling the federal government at every opportunity, courtesy of public welfare. I grew up with my mother in the system. And I grew up in the type of poverty neighborhoods where welfare is king, and the people slumber under him for generations. I grew up seeing every play on the welfare trick in the book, and still see the same shit being done today.

Now because the feds are wise to this, they do try to crack down on the abuse. The problem is that they have no way to really track what many of these people are doing with their benefits. So the only workable solution is to restrict benefits, and complicate the process by which benefits are initiated and distributed. This of course is where the crippling effect comes in. The small percentage of people who need and deserve help, don't get what they need. And the large percentage of hustlers and addicts who work the system, get what they want, a hustle, even a small one counts to them. And sadly enough, these are the people who complain the most.

You see people living on welfare and living in housing projects for generations because of this, where it should only be a few years at best. People learn to sit tight and hold out their hand instead of using their hand to pull themselves out. It should not be that your grandma, great grandma and all your aunts, uncles and cousins live in the same complex. And since this becomes a generational thing, then what you end up doing is raising a generation of *citizen consumers*. These are people whose only purpose in life is to spend money on consumer goods. They spend money that is not earned, but given to them to keep them where they are because often they are no good anywhere else. And sadly the ones that are good go unnoticed because of it. These people in turn are angry at the system, when they should be angry with their neighbors for abusing a system designed to help them.

I'll tell you what. In case any congressman out there with an interest in welfare reform happens to be reading this, I'm going to give you one for free.

Here is how to cut down some of this wasted cost. Where you lose the most is with addicts selling their food-stamps. Now I know that the actual stamps themselves, (department of agriculture greenback from the old days) has been eliminated and replaced with a swipe card. But that swipe card can still be traded. Some crack-head lets someone "borrow" the card along with the pin number for a fee of .50 cents on the dollar towards the value of the card, person X goes shopping, gives the card back later. Welfare knows this happens, so they put a limit on how many cards you can get in a period, with the assumption that captain crack-head will lose or forget his card. He does not; he is burned out but not so foolish as to give up his hustle so easily.

So here is what you do. You make legislation that requires all of the swipe cards to be replaced and modified as an official form of identification. The card for all intensive purposes will become a legal form of I.D. with a photo, name, address, and card number. This card will be recognized by the individual states government as a legal form of identification same as a drivers license. The card will also be a swipe card, which the cashier will swipe for the shopper so that they may examine it, and the shopper will enter their pin from the checkout line.

What this will do. This will not stop the problem, but it will fix a fair percentage of the waste. No person buying a food-stamp card wants to shop with a crack-head, and no crack-head has the patience to actually shop. I predict up to a 20% overall savings on wasted funds. And when you are talking billions in welfare dollars, 20% is a lot. Give it a try, it can't cost any more than the system that is already in place.

Human Interest Stories

In case you haven't figured it out yet, I am not very interested in the lives of humans, and I do not want to hear their stories. Human interest stories flood the news because it distracts us from the news. This is how they make us feel like everything in life isn't completely hopeless. They don't want you to think too hard about some war or some other mess, so they tell you about some lady who builds statues of cats out of tinfoil and bubblegum sticks after the story. I don't care. I don't want to hear it. All that shit is just filler, if they got straight to the point the news would take like eight minutes. So and so is dead, some city got bombed, here is tonight's lottery numbers and tomorrows weather, eight fucking minutes. They need to fill it out so they can justify their advertising time.

The News

And since we are on the subject, I don't like the news anyway. News media is garbage. They don't want to really inform you about anything. They want to captivate you by either shocking you or scaring you with exaggerated information. "Flu X may wipe out the entire population of North America! It has already killed a horse and three sparrows in the last two years!" This kind of news is bullshit. Always over exaggerated, always over dramatized, and never what it's made out to be. Then if something big does happen, you find out too late anyway.

And let's not forget weather prediction. People, it's called "prediction" for a reason. It is an educated guess because they do not actually know what will happen. It takes a pretty thick headed individual to get angry at a meteorologist because it was five degrees hotter than you thought it would be. Grow up. You want to know the weather? Look out of the fucking window.

I don't watch TV. So obviously I don't watch the news either. And I don't read the paper. Newspapers are even more boring than news on television, and they are dirty and they smell. I'd rather make my own news than watch someone else's boring drivel.

The Music Industry

The music industry is amazing. I say this because no place else has the human population been deliberately and obviously sectioned up for the purpose of organized profit. People are a great big pie, and the music industry has sliced that pie up so perfectly it defies description.

One slice is rap, one slice is country, and one slice is rock, and so on and so on. And it's not even that cut and dry, the slices are subdivided even further and sliced even thinner. These slices are portioned perfectly to feed music executives with your money, and you give it up willingly.

These people not only tell you what is popular, they tell you who is popular and for how long, they tell you what to wear based on what music you listen to, what to watch and how much to spend. This is absolutely amazing. It is so amazing to me that people are so brainwashed by this system. There are so many people that will not even listen to another genre of music because they think they are not supposed to. This is the apex of stereotyping. They can plainly see that certain types of music are targeted to specific groups, right down to race and even religion, and allow themselves to be subjected to it. People cloud their own judgment and understanding while continuing to plug more money into a system that they know is designed to keep them in the box. If you don't believe me, go and count how many white rappers and black country western singers are on the charts. Yet black people listen to country, and white people listen to rap. Think about it.

And let's not forget the performers of this music, (I am reluctant to call them artists, few of them deserve the title). These people are disposable to the music industry, and they want it that way. You watch all these trash videos and you think these performers have all this money and an exciting lifestyle, they don't. It's a lie. It's a video and it is as false as everything else on television. It is done to keep your attention and to keep the performers guessing, and clinging because they know that with one slip, they will end up where they were found to begin with. It is rare for someone to actually become a superstar, and rarer still for them to stay there.

Public School

Public school is a mistake that has turned into a multibillion dollar money pit. It simply doesn't work, and everyone knows it. The whole idea behind it is to basically force feed a rounded education into every citizen so that we will not be a race of Neanderthals. Not too much emphasis on any particular subject, just a mouthful of each so people don't grow up too stupid. The premise is a good idea, but it simply doesn't work. Public school has turned into an institution that is better described as crowd control or glorified babysitting.

Here's the problem, you cannot force someone who does not want to learn to get an education. But since it is a law that all children go to school, that is exactly what we do. The schools are full of tens of thousands of kids who don't give a flying fuck about getting educated and simply go through the motions up until they are old enough to walk, or are given their walking papers, and by that I mean their token diplomas.

There are too many adjustments made in order to graduate people who have not earned it. They receive fixed grades from relaxed work that makes it pointless for them to have been there in the first place. All this is done to make everything look Kosher on paper. And that is so that schools will continue to receive funding. This is encouraged and enabled because of IEP's, (individual educational plans) and screwed up kids and honestly dumb kids, are worth more to the schools that receive additional funding to help sort out the rejects who either don't want to be there, or shouldn't be there.

This is not entirely the systems fault. The system is in place the way it is being operated because you have allowed it. You have allowed it to become the monster that now exists by your lack of interest, you lack of involvement, and your lack of discipline where your children are concerned. In keeping with the traditional behavior of the human race, everyone is looking for someone else to handle their responsibility. Parents were not doing their jobs properly, so more responsibility was shifted to the schools. The schools can't handle it because they cannot handle the children; they are not their parents and cannot punish them appropriately. When the schools attempt punishment, the parents complain about it because they feel their rights have been violated. They do so forgetting that they have given up their rights. Either that, or they are actually afraid of confronting their child because the situation has gotten that far out of control. But at the same time the schools don't want to step on the parents toes, simply because they don't want a lawsuit. A lawsuit means lost jobs because the city government is not fit to take responsibility either. Not while they can use teachers for scapegoats. Not that it is so easy to get rid of a teacher, even a bad one has enough tenure to anchor themselves to their job indefinitely.

What we need is a magnet system that lets students test into higher grades and specialize in particular fields or subjects within those grades. A student who is not that smart can transfer to a vocational facility and learn to work with their hands instead of their heads. That is what they want anyway, so why not give it to them? It beats having them hang around in the streets until they end up dead or in jail.

Now I am not saying that education is not important and that effort should not be made, but for God's sake know when to throw in the towel. It is costing billions of wasted dollars yearly for us to force kids that are either too dumb or don't give a shit! The ones who really fall behind are the ones who are intelligent and want to learn and cant because fucked up kids are distracting them and burning up public funding in the process! And this is also where your equality argument comes up again. Many gifted children are overlooked because it would be considered a form of favoritism to provide for their superior intellects. The dumb kids would feel left out…

Fortune Tellers

Telling your fortune, telling your future, reading your palm, tarot cards, unlocking the secrets of the universe in the bottom of a teacup, I'll keep it simple, it's all bullshit. It's con artists telling you what you want to hear so they can scam you out of some cash. And you are all fools for believing it. Any resemblance between what you are told and real life is purely coincidental.

And the biggest sham of all? Zodiacks! What a load of shit this stuff is. All that astrological prediction stuff is a straight con. Just more snake oil salesmen telling you what you want to hear. What's that you say? But your zodiac sounds a lot like you? Of course it does, it sounds a lot like everybody. It's been written that way on purpose. You could read every zodiac in any paper every day and they all will have something that sounds like it may pertain to you because they are written to be very general that way. If you couldn't see what sign they were for you couldn't tell them apart.

The Elderly

Well okay, just to be fair let me point out that I don't mean everybody who is old. There are a lot of nice old folks out there, but there is also a nice bunch of miserable elderly cocksuckers out there who make life hell for everybody they come in contact with. These people are the ones who either didn't do anything they set out to in life or are in terrible pain or are decrepit because they never took care of themselves either.

Like most humans, they seek to take out their anger on everyone and everything because it is more convenient to blame everybody else for everything rather than to take any blame for things that are their own fault. They are close to death, failing in health, in pain, forgetful, and lived meaningless lives, so they are angry. But rather than trying to make a difference, (they say it's never too late, there is some truth to this) they lash out at everyone and try to make other people as miserable as they are. I hope I'm not that angry when I get older…

David Gudgeon

Self Righteous Doctors

If there is anything I cannot stand, it is a doctor that thinks they are higher on the food chain than you are because of a piece of paper. They either look down at you like a laboratory experiment, or they patronize you like you are a little kid, which is essentially the same thing, a superiority complex.

I have had a lot of clashes with doctors over the years for various reasons. I am usually stereotyped as a "patient", and treated as such. I am no average patient. I know my body and thanks to the nature of my childhood I have a very high pain threshold. Doctors of course are used to the wimpy whiney uneducated masses clogging up the emergency room. Not that you can find the actual doctor in the emergency room, not right away anyhow. The fully expect you to beg for painkillers and exaggerate any pain tenfold in typical emergency room drama queen fashion. This I will not do. They also expect for you to be entirely clueless as to why you are actually there, as far as they are concerned, you have no problem at all. At least not until they discover it for you. I have had these experiences in the hospital too many times to overlook the phenomenon.

Scam Email

Bad enough that most of the email I receive is junk-mail and advertisements, do I have to get hit so often with these shitty brainless scams as well? I have to wonder at the sheer stupidity of the human race seeing some of the scams that drop into my email and spam-mail daily, knowing that they would not keep coming if they didn't work on someone. Some idiot somewhere is opening their email right now and thinking that they won a contest or that some banker in Bangladesh needs them to help him divert millions of dollars in misplaced funds. They are wiring these scam artists money, (and I use the term "scam artist" very loosely, some of these emails are painfully obvious) and deserve to lose every penny for being so fucking idiotic as to believe that shit in the first place. I mean really, most of the emails aren't even spelled properly. They are so obviously badly thrown together, without thought or care at all. And yet, there are people who believe them still. So go ahead, waste your money on a scam, you'll probably only throw it away on something else stupid anyway.

Vulgar Comedians

Interesting trend over the last couple of decades that comedians don't have to think in order to entertain a crowd anymore. It used to be that a comedian would have a philosophical approach that would make a crowd laugh, but leave them thinking. Now they make a crowd laugh, and you leave not knowing what was said for the last two hours. And by vulgar comic I don't mean *Benny Hill* vulgar. *Benny Hill* was vulgar at times, but his humor had a storyline to it, and it was funny and original.

Basically what I am saying is that any idiot can cuss and swear and make vulgar lewd sexual comments and get a rise out of an audience because the average person, (particularly the unintelligent person) will laugh at just about anything if it seems nasty. Especially when you get a large group and in the tradition of monkey see monkey do, portions of the crowd will react to the reaction of the rest of the crowd. So you could be too smart for the comments being made, but the primitive side of you still responds to the mob rule.

Unfortunately it seems that the days of comedians like Bill Cosby and George Carlin are gone, and all we are left with are so called funny men who wise crack about *yo mammas ass*. I can't stand it. I have actually sat through some of these concerts without a reaction at all. This mindless vulgarity approach to comedy is slow witted, childish and predictable. You know you are in trouble when *I* can sit there and predict the punch line before the comedian has figured it out themselves. You would think the target audience was twelve years old, and in a way it is. As it seems the average persons mentality is locked into prepubescent adolescence anyway. What a way to evolve…

The Radio

If there was ever a technology that has nearly outlived its usefulness, this is it. The only purpose it serves anymore is to keep long distance drivers awake at the wheel. That is unless you happen to like being told what your favorite songs are and listening to them over and over again with constant interruptions telling you about how they don't interrupt the broadcast with commercials, then they interrupt the broadcast with commercials. And some of the worst, boring, stupid advertising you will find is likely on the radio. That is, if you can keep the station tuned in at all. Sometimes you would have better luck communicating with the space shuttle on a ham radio.

And please don't tell me about satellite radio and that they don't have commercials. Give them time. Just remember the promise of cable television when it first came out. I'm paraphrasing here because it's been a long time, but as I recall the original cable advertising when they were first coming on strong in the early 80s had this slogan, "on cable you will never see a commercial, because you pay for it". Bullshit! It didn't take long to break that promise. With cable you pay for absolutely everything! I'm surprised they haven't figured a way to charge you for flipping channels, (yet).

Music Videos

Just like with cable and video games, I am of the era that came up with the introduction of the music video. I was there when it all started, and it was great. Music videos in the old days, (has it been that long?) had flair, finesse, and often enough some sort of storyline that you could follow in order to make it more interesting.

A music video either looked like a scene from out of a musical, (like Billy Joel's Uptown Girl), or it told a story, (like Michael Jackson's Thriller) this was good stuff and it was interesting and fun to watch. But that was then…

Now the formula is whatever can be done the cheapest. Nobody wants to invest in a good video anymore. They want it cheap and fast, and why not? The so called star of the video is not likely to be recognized or even remembered five years from now, and that is how these companies want it. Disposable performers in cut rate videos, and who gives a shit? The kids are going to buy into it anyway, so why waste money on it? Have rapid clips of some nitwit badly lip sinking a relatively mediocre song into a camera while showing off cars and houses that are probably studio property alongside scantily clad women shaking their asses. In other words, a really cheap production to advertise garbage. What happened to the good videos?

And I'll throw you a bone here to exercise your judgment. Did you ever notice how in videos they cut frame so much while the singer is dancing? That's because many of them cannot dance. They film in dozens of segments because they learn and perform the dance routine in bits. These are not professional dancers, they are musical entertainers. I would be shocked to find that any of your average singers graduated dance at Julliard.

High Heels

I know, I'm being really petty here, but I don't like high heeled shoes. High heels are not good for posture, they degrade muscle structure, they are dangerous to balance and permanently deform the feet when used extensively. And personally, I find them unattractive, (and more personally, I prefer really tall socks, like over the knee high, go figure).

Once upon a time in the 60s a lot of women's groups used to try to make a point by burning bras, this was a mistake. Bras serve a purpose for the woman's body by providing support to the breasts. High heels are a fetish item, generally preferred and encouraged by males. Did you ever see a woman in a strip club dancing in flats? They should have kept their bras on and burned their fucking shoes.

Make-Up

No, I don't like make-up either. I think it makes women unattractive. It is sticky, oily, blotchy, and it has an unpleasant chemical odor. Woman wear make-up because they believe it makes them more attractive, it does not. It hides them behind a mask, it is a lie. And they are lying mostly to themselves. They wear it because they have low self esteem and think they are unattractive without it. They wear it in excess because the use of it becomes desensitizing and the user has to apply more and more in order to feel as if they are getting the same effect.

Make-up is also bad for the skin, and long term use can wear down the skin giving the appearance of premature aging. So what's the solution? Apply more make-up to hide the premature aging, how smart is that?

Shoppers Advantages

Shoppers advantages, savings cards, whatever you want to call them, they can get pretty annoying. I am sick of being forced to join some companies club so I can save on discounts that should be offered freely to the customers anyway in a false effort to make the consumer feel as if they are special or exclusive. What a load. All this is is a way for the company to weasel out of offering discounts to the unsuspecting customer so they can absorb the difference. And if you do join, then you are on the mailing list and they can irritate you with advertisements from themselves and their partners.

Heroes

Let's just get this straight right now, *hero*, is a <u>very abused word</u>. I have grown weary of how easily this word is tossed about by the media. Everyone is not a hero who is viable for news broadcasts or commercialization. I am sick of it. A ballplayer hitting a homerun is not a hero. A guy who falls off his boat and narrowly escapes a shark is not a hero. A reporter in a war zone where he has no business being because he dreams of a Pulitzer is not a hero. Little 5 year old Suzie coaxing a cat out of a tree is not a fucking hero, get it?!? We live in a world where household pets are more heroic than the people who own them.

You are not automatically a hero because you are a police officer, a fire fighter, a paramedic, a teacher, an astronaut, a reporter, a sports VIP, or a soldier. Titles and trivialities do not a hero make. And you certainly are not a hero for doing your job or saving your own sorry ass in an emergency. The hero is the person who runs into danger even though they don't have to, and they are likely completely terrified when they do. And they expect no reward or praise for their actions. They do it because someone else needed their help and doing the right thing was more important than their own life in that moment.

That is why a hero is given a medal or a reward of some sort, to show appreciation for being the hero in the midst of a herd of zeros trampling them underfoot in an effort to run the other way. There would be no rewards for heroic acts if everyone acted heroically. But then they wouldn't be needed.

Patriotism

Or more specifically, *artificial patriotism*. This is patriotism that people present in order to appear as if they are patriotic, or to convince other people because they are afraid of their reactions. It is also done by people to convince themselves they are participating in patriotism so that they can feel important and involved. Waving a flag or painting your mailbox red white and blue does not make someone patriotic. Shouting at a rally or writing a song does not make someone patriotic. Saying a pledge filled with words that many cannot spell or define is not patriotic. Voting, is not patriotic.

Willingly marching to your death because you believe that your life is not as important as the protection of your country and its people, even if you do not fully understand why, is patriotic. It's so funny that when it's time for all these self proclaimed patriots to reach for a gun, they grab a picket sign instead.

Protestors

Protestors are people who want something to change, so they complain. They gather in large groups, obstruct traffic and business, get in people's faces, whip up trouble and vie for media attention to their cause. Sometimes this is a good thing. Coal miners back in the old days picketing because of extreme long hours and deadly working conditions makes sense. Gandhi and Dr. King protesting because of unfair treatment makes sense too. But many protestors are griping about shit that is not that big of a deal, things that only concern them personally. And they get attention because they are annoying, because the media loves it, and because officials want them to shut up. Thus, these people get what they want without earning it or deserving it.

Protestors do not have the knowhow, intelligence or support to effect a change in anything. So they whine and gripe to someone else and try to coax them into doing it. They are selfish, and lazy, wanting other people to do their dirty work for them. And they know if they cry about something long enough, someone will give it to them because society has learned to grease squeaky wheels instead of replacing them.

Artificial Self Esteem

This is a new trend that has really been rearing its ugly head within the last couple of decades. You see, somewhere along the line some people in government finally figured out that a large portion of the population was stupid. It was determined that the problem must be that people have low self esteem. The proposed solution to this problem was to convince people that they had self esteem, even if they didn't, and particularly if they didn't deserve it. And this folks is where a lot of the politically correct terminology and language that we now endure comes from.

I guess the idea is that fake self esteem is better than none at all. But in reality, this just makes the situation worse. Just like love and respect, self esteem is something that must be earned. You earn it by failure. You fail and you fail and then you either finally get it right and finally master it, or you move on to another project and become an expert at that. You do not wake up one day and just feel really good about yourself; just the same way you do not wake up one day and know how to do some skill you never knew before. It takes many years of practice and development to master most things, and this is how it should be. If we could simply plug a program into ourselves and wake up with a new skill, we would never appreciate it. It must be worked for and it must be earned.

You cannot convince children that they are going to be successful by telling them that they are when they are not. That is a lie, and it does not help. It makes things worse. The child may be stupid, but not so stupid that they do not know what they are while you are trying to convince them that they can be anything. They cannot. Everyone cannot be everything that they want to be. If that were the case, the world would be full of nothing but millionaire rock'n'roll astronaut basketball stars and platinum label rapper football MVP's with private islands as home addresses. It doesn't happen that way.

It is okay to lose, and we will lose often. It is humbling and that is necessary to the human condition. It is also the natural way to learn to succeed and to strive for success. We have to learn to accept that fact again or we are doomed as a society.

Political Correctness

To be politically correct is to use feel good language to describe things in life in order to avoid as much as possible any sort of conflict with anyone anywhere who may be potentially the least bit offended by something you may say or imply. This is foolish. This is the governments way of attempting to please all of the people all of the time in order to avoid embarrassments and lawsuits.

What it really does is give people more of an excuse to whine when they don't get what they want or get things the way they want them. It also gives people an excuse to unnecessarily attack people when they don't deserve it in order to stir up trouble in order to create a more favorable situation for themselves.

Politically correct language is a shameless lie, or more appropriately equivocation designed to mask what is being said to protect people's delicate feelings. People are not that delicate. If I was shaken to the core every time someone threw a threat, insult or racial slur at me I would never accomplish anything in life. I don't give a shit what anybody thinks of me or what I say, but I am concerned about when people as a society are slowly being convinced that they can't say anything. This is a very dangerous connotation.

This would be to propose the idea of *thought police*. It is already happening and little is being done about it. I am not talking about the censorship of music, television or art when I suggest this. What I mean is how every time someone says some off color remark anymore they are forced to make a public apology, resign from their job or are sued for it. This sort of action makes other people afraid to express an opinion. That is thought policing.

Nobody should be afraid to speak their mind no matter how crazy they sound or how insulting it may seem. And nobody who slips and says something off-color because they were angry and were spouting off at the mouth without thinking should be persecuted as aggressively as I have seen in recent years. We are a stupid people and we say stupid things. I would be more worried about these people who pretend to be perfect to gain public support. Besides, some people are just jerks, so let them be that way if they want. If you don't like it, you don't have to listen.

Organized Politics

You had to have seen this one coming. I don't like anything else, why would I lay off of politics? I do not like organized politics and I do not trust career politicians. By organized politics I mean when politicians work together on subjects they have no business in or on subjects that they should be against in order to hold onto their offices or in order to push through a bill or some other such thing that they know will get stonewalled without some sort of *cooperation* on their part.

And by career politicians I mean anybody who makes themselves a politician on purpose and by choice not to help the people, but as a career choice because they like the idea of being wealthy, popular and powerful. This is becoming a great problem because there are too many people in politics now who fall into the category of *celebrity politicians*. And I do not mean former celebrities who become politicians, I mean politicians who so crave the attention of their office that they manufacture themselves into false celebrities. Camera hogs that show up for every ribbon cutting and make talk show appearances to make sure that people can see their face as often as possible. These are false celebrities who are famous for being famous, and for the most part, never really seem to have done much of anything aside from get press.

Additionally to this category, is the *mascot-politician*. This individual is also a celebrity, but one who has been manufactured by other members of their party as opposed to being self made. These people are effectively on display to show the good side of a party, or to somehow display change by the party. These people are generally inexperienced, are totally party oriented, but tend to have a dynamic personality. They get press coverage where none is needed and awards that were neither earned nor deserved. The *mascot* is often a born and bred politician whose ambitions have always been political. They are excellent equivocators and even better orators. In other words; great representation for the party, great smokescreen for the people. Or as Douglas Adams so eloquently put it, *"His job is not to wield power but to draw attention away from it"*, (From The Hitchhiker's Guide To The Galaxy). These types of politicians are the most dangerous, as they whip the people into a frenzy against anyone with enough intelligence to challenge their frequent mistakes. Politicians like this cannot handle criticism very well and tend to either attack it or convince others to do it for them. They respond this way because they are often so used to posh lives and yes men constantly stroking their egos. They rarely have a real-world understanding of pain, discomfort or hardships as they have rarely or never experienced them. The frightening part here is that this type is the most obvious, yet the masses refuse to see it because they are being told what they want to hear and being given a scapegoat for which to place the blames of their troubled lives. They believe blindly if they have someone to blame for their troubles, even if they never or hardly ever see results from their candidate of choice.

From what I have seen of history, (not just American history) the best politicians, presidential, congressional, kings or otherwise were and are the ones who didn't want the job. They took it out of obligation because they thought they had the leadership skills to help the people they became in charge of and tried to make a difference. They put themselves on the line and got their hands dirty and took responsibility for what they said and did even if it made them look bad or foolish or cost them their lives. That is honorable. If you screwed up, admit it, go on and so be it. But what I see now is not honorable. It is cowardly and self motivated. Politicians who snivel about every little thing and grovel for apologies for things that offend the press, fuck that. Politicians who make millions on the side and formulate questionable deals, (nothing wrong with making some change) but straight up dirty dealing, fuck that too. Politicians who pretend to give a shit about the people's concerns because it looks good in newspaper print and yet do nothing about them because they vote with the party so they can stay down with their boys instead of what their conscience tells them, and despite what their districts want or need. Fuck that three times over.

And if by some chance you happen to be a politician reading this, I hope that this passage doesn't apply to you. If it does, try and remember the proper definition of your title, perhaps it's not too late to make a difference. And if this passage does apply to you, well, <u>fuck you</u>!

Voice Recognition Software

Whoever invented this type of programming must have really hated people to design such a system that seems so useful, and is yet so terribly frustrating. Imagine, as you read this millions of people the world over are screaming at their phones in frustration because the Voice Recognition program on the other end of the line holding their credit card information hostage cannot understand their accents or tone of voice and won't transfer the call. What happened to the good old days when you just punched in your numbers? I do not want to recite fifty numbers only to have a machine tell me it does not understand me, and then put me on hold for half an hour so I can talk to some operator at the companies call station in Ecuador who I can't understand!

Censorship

Censorship is a good idea and a bad one at the same time. There are many things that should be kept from the eyes and ears of young people simply because they are not yet of an age of understanding, because they have not developed enough cognitively to properly comprehend what they see and hear. They can become easily desensitized to the wrong things and misinterpret much of what they see, and can be affected for life as a result.

But often an attempt to control media and art is disguised as censorship, and art as a result is abused and strangled out of its creativeness. This is an effort towards forced conformity. On the other end, you have overly concerned individuals trying to shield young people from what they should not have access to in the first place. But they would not be in a position to do this to begin with if you had not given them the power to do so.

Censorship should begin at home. If there is something that you are sure that your child should not be watching, then don't let them watch it. They can see it when they are older and are better equipped to understand it. Wimpy parents who do not want to confront their own children because of a lack of understanding in how to deal with their children are responsible for the government and other agencies enforcing censorship. Parents have passed the buck onto such organizations out of sheer laziness. They want a fortune spent by the government to parent their children, and then whine about taxes, if they pay them at all. They complain about their children's behavior, but overreact when someone else tries to discipline them, even though they will not do it themselves. They expect the school to parent their children, and then take away the teachers authority, thus making teachers authority figures without the ability to enforce any sort of authority because they in turn are afraid the parents will complain about it, in order to once again avoid confronting the children. This sort of problem is also pressed into law enforcement. There are too many officers who can hardly do their jobs because they have to make nice to try and keep from offending someone. Pathetic…

And before you say anything, remember, I don't watch television. I do not have cable in my home. I have a DVD collection of movies and TV shows so I know exactly what the children watch in my house and how much they watch of it at all times.

So in short, censure your own rotten foul children and stop expecting everyone else to do it. There would be no need for others to do it if you did your jobs as parents. And quit complaining about censorship being enforced when it is your own fault. When you lay off, they will stop.

Sameness

Yes, we are living in the age of the sameness generation. Everywhere you go, everything is the same now. Try this exercise, drive across America. Just get in the car and drive from state to state. If you don't happen to notice the signs welcoming you to the new state, you will not even know you have crossed the border, (if there is a sign, I have done this and found many states without them anymore). Every state I drove into had the same restaurants, the same gas stations, the same retail outlets and all arranged the same way and looking identical. Once upon a time the signs on the businesses were the same, but the buildings looked different, not anymore. Now the buildings are the same for the same establishments from state to state, and are even laid out the way same in many instances. In fact, the only things that do look different are these massive city sized casinos that have been cropping up in various parts of the country. Some of these casinos are so big they look like the backdrop from a sci-fi movie. And all these housing communities that are cropping up look the same too. These little compacted manufactured suburban enviro-camps with hundreds of identical houses laid out on grids right next to shopping malls that look like every other shopping mall. It used to be that you knew a difference by the landscape, but we are slowly erasing it. Finding a beautiful unmarred, unmarked landscape is getting harder to do. We are supposed to tame the earth, not destroy it. If we destroy it, it will destroy us by default because we can't live without it.

Spay/Neuter Your Pet

I love my pet, so I am going to slice off his balls? Not so cute when you put it like that, is it? But that's exactly what it is. People want to own something that they shouldn't own because they are too irresponsible to own them in the first place. People do not want to keep track of their animals, and they do not want to be responsible for extra little animals, so they have their pet mutilated. They want their pet to be more docile without the responsibility of training, so they have their pet mutilated. Once again, humans manage to find the easy way out. It is very selfish to want to <u>own</u> a living thing and then not take care of it once you have effectively enslaved it to satisfy the emotional deficit in your life.

Holidays

I do not like holidays. All of the holidays are either made up events or mangled and manipulated events perpetrated by advertisers in order to sell a product or boost sales in a particular time slot. I am sick of this. Why does someone else get to decide what day I show affection to or purchase a gift for someone I care about? Why do I need to be put under pressure to purchase a gift for someone? Why do they need to be put under pressure to purchase something for me? Enough already! What does a chocolate Easter Bunny have to do with Jesus anyway? I don't see little kids eating chocolate Apostles and hunting for candy Easter nails. No fun in that, so it's not profitable. And don't tell me about eggs representing the rebirth, those eggs will never hatch. If I boiled a refrigerated egg and it hatched a chick, then I would go to church...

Pharmaceutical Companies

I am tired of pills being the answer to everything. What happened to good old fashioned willpower? What happened to people believing in themselves and fighting their cravings? What happened to people toughing up against things that were uncomfortable and overcoming them on their own? Now there's a pill for goddamn everything.

You take a pill because you are lactose intolerant and too stubborn to give up the dairy because you like the taste despite the upset stomach. You would rather risk your health and take a pill than not eat something that harms your body. The pill has a side effect, let's say diarrhea, so you take a pill for that. Then another side effect causes nausea, so you take another pill for that. The nausea pill causes headaches, for which there is a pill, whose side effect is upset stomach. Back to square one, but never fear, there's a pill for that too.

Are you all fucking stupid? Can you not see the long term damage of all this medication? You should hold out as long as possible to avoid the use of medications. Let your body sort it out if it can. And if you are in pain, fuck it! Tough it out! You were made of stronger stuff than that. Quit being weak and throw the pills out. You are being set up by companies who make billions off of your hypochondria. Whatever your problem is, they will make a pill for it because a pill is a shortcut, and most humans will always migrate towards the low road.

You should all be ashamed of yourselves for letting it get this bad. All this medication is used to squeeze profit from you, and to control you. There are so many mood and mind altering drugs floating around, particularly with our youth, simply as a form of crowd control. Nobody wants to deal with you or your kids, so they give them a pill. Shuts them right up and makes them codependent for life, thus controlling them for life and keeps the money coming.

Once upon a time torture was used to control ill people, then imprisonment, then lobotomies, then electroshock, now pills. All the other methods are now considered barbaric, 200 years from now what will future people say about our abuse of medications? Will there be anyone left to say anything in 200 years? Or will we poison ourselves out of existence?

Organized Religion

I have nothing against people believing whatever they choose to believe. I have nothing against belief in God or a higher power whatever it may be. What I do have a problem with is people who believe something and are hell bent on turning you over to it. I also have a problem with people telling you what to believe, how to believe it and how to worship it if worship is required, (or even if it's not).

People do not want to hear that what has been written in their scripture or in their respective bible may be only stories. They absolutely have to believe it because they do not believe in themselves enough to hold their faith without some tangible form to cling to. A book with old stories becomes tell all and see all because to have faith without something physical is faith without telling and seeing. This is not faith based believing. If you believe something that is spiritual in nature then you should not need physical evidence to back it up, you simply believe.

Furthermore, you do not need to force other people to believe what you believe if they do not believe as you do. This is an attempt to self justify your own so called faith in something because you doubt yourself. If you really believe, then you don't care what other people think about it. But most people will become irate and angry when challenged; this is a sign of weakness, ignorance or low intelligence.

This is one of the main reasons that there has been so much bloody conflict all throughout written history and beyond pertaining to religion. I could go on all day about how almost every war in history has some sort of religious attachment, whether it was fighting over the religion itself, or religion was only an excuse to justify slaughtering thy neighbor. It is a well known fact that much war has been waged over how to worship the same god, or how to force one culture to adopt the god and practices of another.

You will find also that the writings in which people believe are often filled with radical inconsistencies which are denied by people when confronted with them. They refuse to see the lack of logic in what they believe and take metaphoric meanings as literal ones. There are far too many examples to even seriously touch on this subject in writing such as presented here. On that note, I strongly recommend reading "*The Age Of Reason by Thomas Paine*" as an example of research into inconsistencies and illogic within historical religious writing.

Nevertheless, as I have said, people can believe whatever they want, just don't cram it down my throat. I don't want to hear it. Religion is all too often manipulated to control people, and habitually abused for profit. It takes advantage of the meek who are looking to quell their fears about what happens after this life. Truly the mysteries of the afterlife are an answer that no human that I have ever heard of could or can answer with any realistic certainly or accuracy.

People are so subconsciously scared that they do not really believe what they think they believe, that they have to convince other people to believe it with them to justify their acceptance in their so called faith. They are transposing their belief onto someone else so they can feel that they are not alone in what religion they follow. Or they pretend to believe because others believe it, and they are afraid of persecution because people enforce what they believe so strongly. And they enforce it out of fear.

People also seek out religion in order to discover spirituality, but religion and spirituality are not the same thing. Spirituality is a condition of mind that you feel and experience cognitively and emotionally, it is not a physical thing. Religion is an attempt to make something spiritual into something physical. This is akin to bottling sunlight. Spirituality is found within, and religion is found without, and is often <u>without</u> spirituality. One may use religion to seek spirituality, and they may find it in a dream or on a mountaintop. They seek it never knowing where it really is because it is with them the whole time. They must discover it within themselves and no church of any denomination can do this. If you found it in a church, or with a religion, you still found it within yourself, just in a different physical place if you really found it at all.

Many intelligent religious leaders take advantage of these fears and quests for the soul so they may exploit them for money and power. They encourage a flock because a flock is a group of sheep. The trick with sheep is like flocks of birds and schools of fish they all easily are turned in the same direction. A shepherd not only keeps the flock safe, sometimes he shears them, and sometimes he leads them to slaughter as well.

I am no sheep, and neither am I a shepherd.

Things People Have Not Learned

The human race has been around longer than anyone alive today is truly aware of. Written history goes back some thousands of years, and evidence of civilization goes back tens and perhaps even hundreds of thousands of years farther than that. We may have inhabited this planet for millions of years for all we know, and could have had civilizations rise and fall inside of various global disasters such as ice ages and meteor strikes for example.

In all of this time, people have learned, (and unlearned) many things valuable and otherwise. But most of what we have learned has been technical, that is, the development of machines, cultivation and more recently, large scale industrialization and electronics. In all of this time and with all of these advances, there are still some things that the human race has never really learned on a large scale. Our emotional and spiritual development is seriously lacking, and it holds us back.

Moderation

People as a collective have never really learned moderation. They want everything and too much of it. They are never happy with what they have if someone else has one thing more. They are unwilling to earn it, and are often compelled to steal it or misappropriate it in some way.

When they do have something, they want more and more of it, and they horde it and bury themselves in stuff. People's homes are cluttered with shit they don't want or need so that other people cannot have it. People are like chimpanzees fighting over a spoon because it is shiny. They are like mice cramming their nests with scraps of paper and other odds and ends simply to be doing it. They don't know when too much is enough. Not only with material things but with their own bodies as well. People will eat till they are fit to burst, and eat some more, knowing they are killing themselves and hurting the people around them.

Self Control

People have rarely learned the art of self control. They will overindulge in passions until those passions eventually destroy them. They will allow themselves to become slaves to their desires until their desires are all they know. People have not learned to turn themselves off when they are getting too close to the edge. They have not learned to say no to themselves when they are at risk of harming themselves and others emotionally, financially and physically. They abuse themselves and others, and lash out at other people for their own personal mistakes. They react violently to challenges, both physically and verbally.

Criticism

People are terrible at accepting criticism. You can't tell some people anything without a verbal tirade. People will cuss and argue and shout over you to drown you out rather than even consider that they may be wrong about something. People behave like small children when criticized, and indeed that is just what they are. If a person is raised in such a way that they never learn to deal with someone correcting them or not agreeing with them, then the part of their mind that is associated with that particular function has never fully developed.

Practice What They Preach

People love to go on and on about what is wrong with everybody else, (considering the nature of this book I will have to say present company included and accepting the guilt on this one) but rarely do they ever fit into the molds they suggest. People love to talk about other people because it makes them feel superior. They can pretend to be better than someone else because they have the ability to point out the faults in others. That is why so called reality television has become so popular. It gives couch potatoes the ability to look down their snouts at other people's lives. It makes them feel less worthless to condemn other people, as it is easier to condemn others than change things within ourselves.

Do Unto Others

People often have a very holier than though attitude and want to be treated as such. People want to be treated like kings and queens, but treat other people like crap. They insist on privacy and rights as human beings and citizens, but are rarely concerned when someone else is being violated, particularly if they are the ones perpetrating the violations. They want respect without earning it, and success without achieving it, yet will take these things from others who deserve it without a second thought.

Quality vs. Quantity

Quality vs. quantity is a major issue for people, (and a huge issue with me). They too easily mistake a lot of something cheap as having a value over a single item of great superiority. They fail to see that a lot of something that was inexpensive and made of inferior materials or poor construction will cost them more in the long run than an item of high standards both physically and in assembly that came at an additional cost. This pertains to items that are consumed as well. Eight ounces of real 100% juice is much better for you than 32 ounces of soda, but since you get more of the soda for less, that is what you are likely to drink, even though you know that the soda is not good for your body.

The industrial age has been a big perpetrator in this recently, and that has been magnified by corporations looking for profit. But it is no excuse for people's poor choices. You should all know better, but you make lousy choices.

Integrity

I also see integrity as a big problem. People are liars and spineless as well. They will lie straight to your face about things that don't even concern them because they are afraid or because they want to fire up some mess and watch it burn. They rarely stand up for themselves or anyone else, and when they do it is never for the right reasons. The reasons are often egotistical and self motivated. People will hardly ever take credit for their own wrongdoings, and when they do it is because they are cornered and left with no other option but to fess up. Then they act like it was a big deal that they apologized or told the truth, and expect to be praised for doing the right thing, but have the nerve to be angry with other people who behave the same way.

Individuality

People are masters of acting like individuals by copying everybody else. They don't think for themselves and when they do they think like what is the popular norm. They duplicate what they are told is popular, and then claim to be individual for it. Then they have the nerve to persecute people who truly are acting as individuals because they lack the imagination to understand them or even try. If they had imagination, they could be individual without replicating and rehashing other people's styles.

Make Decisions

People do not like to make decisions because they are afraid they will be wrong. They allow other people to either manipulate them or make suggestions to sway them, or to straight out decide for them. People are afraid of what they do not know, and therefore do not like to change things. Decisions invoke change. What people do not realize when following this spineless practice is that when you cannot or will not make a decision for yourself, someone will do it for you. Although this is what many people desire, it is not always desirable, and the outcome may not be what you think. People making choices for you takes your power. It makes you weak. And you allow it.

Get Over It

People have not learned to get over themselves. They think that they are the all important centers of the universe. The most unique and significant beings in all of existence and that the world will stand completely still without them. They are entitled to everything they want and deserve it fully whether they deserve it or not.

Some people are very important, and all people who make an effort in life have an importance in life, even if it is temporary. But each individual is not the solely most important thing in the universe at any one time. There are other people too, and they are probably better and more deserving than you, so get over it!

Take Care Of Themselves

Most people have never learned to take proper care of themselves. They are fat and lazy and unhealthy. They do not eat right, exercise right, educate themselves right, sleep right, work right or anything else right. They know they are hurting themselves and others, and go right on doing it, no matter how much it hurts. Then they wonder why they feel like shit. It's because they don't want to take the blame for being their own executioners when their health fails them. Then they have the nerve to poke fun of people who take excellent care of their health. They lash out against others with more willpower in typical human fashion.

Take Care Of Others

Obviously, if you can't take care of yourself, you can't take care of anyone else either. People who can barely take care of themselves cannot honestly be expected to take care of children, spouses, pets, friends, houseplants or anything else for that matter. And this is no excuse for them not trying. It is a point that if you don't know what to do to keep yourself going, how can you keep anyone else going in any other way than to set a bad example and hope that others will try to avoid being like you, (like I did with my parents). I am a rare example of someone going in the opposite direction of my upbringing. I can't be the only one, I hope…

Maintain The Environment

We all absolutely must rely upon our environments, both personally and globally for survival. Everything we use originated as a natural source, even artificial things we produce to duplicate the natural started from nature. We pick things up clean, and leave a huge mess behind us every time. When the mess gets too big, we move to another area and tear it down as well. We are like a cancer, devastating the topography as we move about, living in our own filth and trash, while forcing it on our neighbors and demolishing our environment. We do little to replenish what few natural resources we tear down to use, and have the nerve to complain about it. We kill and poison everything we come into contact with, and show no regard as to how it eventually affects us and other life forms that share our planet. By killing our environment, we kill ourselves and our *selective insight* won't let us see it.

Love vs. Lust

We mistake love for lust. Love and lust is not the same thing. Love is not sexual desire. Sexual desire and sexual expression are a part of love, but not love in of itself. This confusion grows out of adolescent promiscuity. Young people who are not emotionally ready for a sexual relationship, but indulge in sexual practices anyway confuse themselves. Many of them come from homes where they never learned to love because their parents never learned it and therefore cannot teach it or show it. Many more are confused because their bodies are ready before their minds are, and there is no-one around with the intelligence to explain the difference.

Sex feels good. Giving and sharing sex as an expression of love can be a wonderful gift. But seeking sex for the purpose of pleasure only is not the same. But when you are young and have never really felt emotional love or even ever been truly happy, someone making you feel really good physically can be misinterpreted. Many young people break their own hearts this way by allowing themselves to be deceived by other young people who only want to get off. They are taken by predators seeking physical gratification. These people in turn never learn the true joy and nature of a natural emotional romantic love, and thus recycle the fault into their own unwanted children who are often conceived and born out of this type of deception. These children are condemned to repeat the mistake. It is sadly rare not to.

Spirituality

Rarely does anyone learn to look inside themselves and truly discover what and who they really are. Rarely does anyone feel a sense of purpose. People do search, but they search in all the wrong places. Very often people turn to religion, but this can be deceptive. Often all it is, is someone telling you what to think about the supernatural, and you accepting it because you lack the imagination or the intellect to interpret it for yourself. You spend your whole life lost without realizing that you are lost within yourself, and that only you can find yourself and set you free.

I'll help you out a little with this one; the first step is to admit that you just don't know. Then admit that as a species, we humans very likely lack the intelligence to fully interpret what we discover. Empty your cup before you fill it.

Civilization

Or better yet, perhaps I should say civilized behavior. People behave like wild animals. People like to pretend that they are civilized because they are concerned with what other people think about them, but this is only vanity and ego. This is *center of the world complex* at its best. People like to pretend that they are all important and all knowing and perfect. So they pretend they are civilized. Then they act like inmates who escaped from a mental institution when they think no-one is looking. If they are found out, they lie about it until evidence is presented, then they make up excuses and seek outside blame for their behavior so they don't have to accept any blame themselves. Hardly civilized behavior…

Respectful

People are really shitty about respecting other people, period. They don't respect other people's opinions, beliefs, religions, ideas, property or persons. They treat each other like garbage, and then demand respect! There is nothing wrong with not agreeing with someone else about what they believe, but respect their right to believe it if they choose. People are often unwilling to give respect until they feel it is earned, I understand this. But very often when they receive it, they don't give it back. This is petty and selfish. Very human indeed.

Virtue

That's right, virtue. Have a set of rules and standards that are fair, honorable, and realistic, and stick to them no matter what. Be honest and upright. Be intelligent and artistic. Be kind and firm. How often do you see that anymore? The Knights tried it and they were either corrupted or persecuted. The Samurai tried it and they were cast out by their own government. The Buddhists tried it and they got thrown out of Tibet. Every time a society tries to angle towards a virtuous direction, they get flattened for it. You should think that productive behavior modification would be a desirable trait. I guess all the defective people get jealous and since they outnumber everyone else, well...

Things That Should Be
Made Into Law

I have a lot of pet peeves, (no shit, right?) and there are a few things that I think should be required of everyone. I suggest certain training or classes or requirements that everyone should be directed into at a certain age. People are too dumb to be left to their own devices, especially where the safety of others are concerned.

It used to be that dumb people would accidentally wipe out other dumb people, and keep the population down, now things are too safe and we are overpopulated. So if they are going to get along in modern society, they may as well do it half-assed right.

Driving

People are lousy drivers. Driving is easy, the mechanism of actually driving has become surprisingly simple, and yet people still cannot do it properly. You see them all day, every day on the roads and highways. People who drive too fast, too slow, merge without signaling, miss stop signs, rip through stop signs, blast their stereos cross over lines and make illegal turns.

Additionally people make really dangerous moves because they are not paying attention. I live in a city where there are many one-ways, I cannot tell you how many times I have had a car flying straight at me because they were the wrong way on a one-way street, and have the nerve to honk and cuss at me like I did something wrong. Drivers are on their cell-phones talking or texting, or they are trying to read or write something while driving. Many people are putting on make-up, eating, or even shaving while driving. People are impatient. It wasn't that long ago that being able to travel even 30 miles an hour was unheard of. People don't appreciate how far this technology has come.

People are stupid and dangerous in their cars. They are unsafe, they don't pay attention and they are unnecessarily aggressive. People don't use their safety belts, they don't secure their children, they overload their cars with passengers, they drive while the vehicle is in need of repair, and drive under the influence of narcotics, medication and alcohol. A car is a big dangerous machine; I don't care how safe the vehicles themselves have become. It only takes one slip to kill yourself or someone else.

I think that anyone seeking a driver's license should be required to take professional training before being allowed to take the driver's test. I think that the days of Uncle Bill or grandma giving driving instruction to a teenager should be abolished. This scenario is an example of the blind leading the blind. How can we expect people who can barely manage the rules of safe driving to teach a teenager who is barely paying attention, (it is in the nature of a teenager to ignore you because they think they know everything). How can we honestly expect them to learn how to drive safely and properly?

You want to cut down on driving fatalities? Actually teach people how to drive.

Rubber Necking

If there is an accident or some emergency the worst thing in the world you can do is stand around watching it. You are keeping the professionals from doing their jobs properly, and lives may be on the line. You could easily end up being responsible for someone's death because you were in the fucking way. Get the hell out of the way and let the people who actually know what they are doing handle it. If that was you laying there you would be appalled at the crowd.

And these idiots who have to drive extra slow and look out the window so they can get some juicy gossip are even worse. I have actually seen more than once another accident occur because people driving by were not looking where they were going so they could get details on an accident they were passing. Serves them right...

Parenting

Now here is a lost art! Fucking parenting! Kids today get knocked up and knocked out and don't know what the hell to do with a child because they are children who grew up with no discipline, understanding or love, and are expected to know how to raise a child. They were raised by rejects who in turn didn't know what they were doing either. Too many parents tried and try to be a child's friend instead of a parent because they want to avoid the confrontation involved with establishing discipline. Either that or they are so overbearing that they become abusive, and torture the child, turning them into another monster for society to deal with. Too many people just don't have the skill it takes to raise a child anymore. This is very sad considering that it is a natural function that we have been practiced in for some hundreds of thousands of years and perhaps longer.

For Gods sakes, cats and dogs seem to treat their young better than we do. It's embarrassing when a species that ranks lower on the food chain is more compassionate than we are. I honestly think that there should be some form of instruction for young pregnant mothers to show them at least proper disciplinary procedures. And those androids that the high schools hand out do not count. A flimsy automaton baby that simulates infancy is no substitute for the real thing. Particularly since most of these girls have a ton of experience raising siblings and cousins already, and likely do it wrong. More realistically, it is very likely that a few of them already have a kid, and the rest of them have had a younger sibling dumped on them for extended periods of time by parents who don't want to deal with their babies.

Gambling Limits

There are restrictions on most narcotics, and limits on alcohol, (not that alcohol limits are ever imposed mind you) but none on gambling. At the very least with alcohol, a responsible bartender may throw your bum ass out if you have had too much to drink. A bartender may even take your keys, but who throws you out of a casino? Nobody, unless you are out of money, but then they give you credit so they can sue you and take your property too.

People waste as much money gambling as is wasted on alcohol, drugs, cigarettes, and any other habit you can think of. But there is no regulation that I know of. And you know why? Because the tax revenue is outstanding! And if people are stupid enough to burn away all of their hard earned money, then fuck-em! That is the attitude.

The problem with that however is that in the process of a gambler destroying themselves, they drag a lot of people down with them. And that is why I think there should be some regulation to shut them down. If you are a drunk or a junkie, they throw your ass in rehab. Rehab hardly ever works, but at least an effort is made. I say embarrass addicted gamblers by throwing them in the tank. If they have the nerve to carry the term addicted like gambling is a disease, then treat them like it and hospitalize their sorry butts!

Dog Training

People like to own dogs. They do not however like to train them. People who do not understand discipline because they are undisciplined, cannot teach it effectively to anyone else, including dogs. If someone has never learned self control from their parents because their parents were wild, they cannot train an animal any more than they can train a child.

Regardless of a dog's pedigree or domestication, it is still an animal. It has close cousins in the wild and accordingly reacts instinctively unless properly trained. An untrained dog lives its whole life essentially as a puppy, and never grows up. It whines and slobbers and snivels and tears up like it's 12 weeks old throughout its adult life. This is neither fair to the dog or the owners, nor is it fair to the neighbors who lay awake at night listening to the animal howl and who get jumped every time they pass the yard. Improperly trained dogs are a nuisance, and if you ever get rid of your dog, it will likely end up euphonized because it cannot be properly controlled.

Do not own a dog, (or any pet) simply to own it. If you cannot or do not know how to take care of it, then you can only abuse the animal. And yes, an untrained animal is abused. Anyone who gets a dog should be required to get it trained.

Noise

Is it just me, or has everything recently gotten really fucking loud? I can hardly hear myself think anymore. Especially on the road, I have been three cars back from people who had their stereos so loud I can feel the vibrations in my teeth. There is too much noise and it is too loud!

Part of the problem is that people are inconsiderate. They want to drown everybody out so they blast the music or the television. These people are fools because they are causing long term permanent damage to their inner ears. The ear is particularly sensitive, and it can only handle so much before it breaks down. The ear canal, (cochlea) may swell with fluid to block noise, so we turn it up louder. The cilia, (little hairs) of the inner ear when stressed break off, and never grow back. That is where hearing loss comes from. And people do it to themselves <u>on purpose</u>.

There are already noise pollution laws in many places, but I rarely hear about them being enforced. Seriously, the noise needs to stop. We are all getting hard of hearing, and there is no peace to be found. Turn all that shit off and go read a book.

Forced Labor

And don't give me any shit about slavery either, just read. Courts already have forced labor, it's called community service. It is where they make you pay your debt to society with sweat equity instead of cash. It is meant to make you give back to the community that you fucked over when you were caught being a prick, and it is also meant to embarrass you in an effort to keep you from repeating the offence, a method that does little for people who have no self esteem to begin with.

Depending upon the crime, I think that most of the lower level criminals should be made to do community service. Drug addicts in particular. Make forced labor part of their treatment plan. God knows it would be nice for them to contribute something back. If most people had any clue what rehabilitation actually cost and then added up the average number of times that an addict is thrown back into a rehab program they would keel over and die on the spot.

Making these people work is likely the worst thing you could do to them anyway. Addicts do not want to work, I promise you. Most addicts are used to pulling down fast money because they need the quick cash to feed the beast. That is why so many of them are thieves and prostitutes. The fear of doing hard labor for the city would probably scare a lot of them straight.

Legal vs. Illegal

People are always trying to turn dumb shit into law. Equally, people are always trying to overturn other dumb shit that is already law. Both of these options are executed by individuals who have a personal interest in the outcome, either because it affects their lifestyle, or they have some potential profit to make on the side.

There are many other things people would like to see enforced or rescinded simply because they are stupid, and don't see the big picture, or any picture.

Marijuana

Boy is this a popular subject. Well I'm not a popular person, so here it comes. Marijuana, the most abused illicit drug *not* on the market. It is the most abused of the illegal drugs because it is one of the cheapest and easiest to obtain. Most people who use it claim also not to, depending on the company that they keep. As it is apparently very easy to get hold of, it is however still illegal, and comes with all the bells and whistles of any other narcotic in its class.

There are many who will tell you that there is nothing serious about its use, and many more who will tell you about long term damage due to its use. What I do know is that when people use it they tend to act even more stupid and lazy than usual. It's like they are paying for an opportunity to act even more useless than normal. And then lacking the capacity to notice how useless and stupid they were, because they were too high at the time to notice. This is sad.

Lots of people are pulling out there for the legalization of marijuana; I think it would be a mistake. People cannot control their indulgences as it is. They smoke till it kills them, they drink till it kills them, and they gamble till they are homeless, so on and so forth. Marijuana would be overused if it were in full legal access to the public. People would end up being more absent minded and lazy, and unemployment would go up. Then more foreigners would take the available jobs, and all the *high* unemployed people would bitch that they lost their jobs to border jumpers. The border jumpers are probably high too, but at least they are smart enough to keep on working.

Furthermore people like to use the example of other countries that are far more relaxed about marijuana laws. In the process of doing so, they avoid talking about other countries that are by American standards amazingly strict about drug laws. Take Brunei for example, where possession will get you death by firing squad. It is for this reason that in 2004 Indonesian authorities reported a bust of 4.2 kilos of marijuana as the largest bust in their history. The obvious reason for this being that people there are terrified to be caught with the stuff.

Alcohol

Looking at how stupid people get with this shit, it's a wonder that it was ever legal to begin with. It is easily abused and comes with a social edge. When I tell people I don't drink they look at me like I have three heads. And if they have had enough to drink, that is probably what they see.

Alcohol is terribly wasteful and abused. Young people like it because it makes them feel older, older people like it because they are used to it. Honestly many of the people I have talked to have said they wish they didn't drink. I hear the same thing about cigarettes all the time. So if people don't want to use it, then why do they? Weak willed, that's why. They allow habit and social pressure to dictate their behavior. Instead of saying, "I don't want to drink tonight" they say, "well, maybe just one" and just one becomes just five.

And don't give me that drivel about it being cultural. Fuck culture. People originally brewed spirits because there was no clean water. The intoxicating effects seemed like a bonus because they were primitive people and didn't know better. But we are aware now of the damage it does when not used in moderation. And since when are humans moderate about anything?

There are many places where alcohol is not and does not seem to have hardly ever been legal. In the Western world however, it is a cultural staple. Because of widespread abuse, Western practices were stifled, for example prohibition in America. This failed. It failed because it was stopped, not because it was not working. All that stuff about gangsters had little to do with it. Bootlegging in those days was no bigger than any illegal drug sales going on today. In fact, it was likely on a far smaller scale than anything you can imagine by today's standards. I don't believe that prohibition was stopped because of gangsters or gunfights or a strain on government spending or anything like it. I have a different idea about what ended it.

Has it ever occurred to anyone that in the same year that the ban on alcohol was lifted the first New Deal went into effect? The new first of the New Deals was official in March of 1933, prohibition ended in December 1933. The New Deal was a massive financial undertaking; the money had to come from somewhere, and the government didn't have any. It was during the Great Depression, unemployment was record high, banks were failing, and the government was running out of money, the people were starving, but they could still manage to scratch up some change for booze? So tax them why don't you! Alcohol sales spelled out fantastic tax revenue, and the money was needed for the new deal projects.

It's what people call a *sin tax*. Why do you think that gambling has slowly been becoming legal? Tax revenue. Why do you think that it is state governments running lotteries? Tax revenue. Should alcohol consumption be controlled? Probably so. Will it happen? Probably not. You could say you are losing a freedom, but who is really free?

Corporal Punishment

I'll just say this right off. If you have a kid that absolutely has lost control it is probably in the best interest of even the child to whack them, if only for shock value alone. Control must be established and discipline must be understood by a child. A child actually desires a measure of control, so that they may learn by example to control themselves. But a child will deliberately test this control, and push the limits of it in some cases. I do not think there is anything wrong with a physical discipline as a last resort if done properly and in moderation.

The problem with corporal punishment comes from parents who have never learned boundaries with physical discipline because no boundaries were used on them. They got the living tar kicked out of them, and reflect that behavior with their children. This is a difficult cycle to break. People often do not realize when they have crossed the line from slapping a little kid on the back of their hand to shock them to attention, and covering them with whelps from an extension cord. That so many parents cannot tell the difference is tragic. But it runs a little deeper than even this.

Many parents abuse these children because they do not know how to control them and because they resent them for supposedly ruining their parents lives with their very existence. They were unwanted, and their presence is a hindrance to what might have been for the parent, at least on some subconscious level to the parent. This one I know from my own childhood experience. But I still think corporal punishment should be allowed, although many people need guidelines as to its application. What is being asked for here is moderation from people who do not understand what moderation means.

Prostitution

Now we're talking! Legal legal legal! Legalize this all the way! If the government were to hit a new sin tax target, this would have to be it. Sex is the one thing that you can claim "*everybody's doing it*" and probably be right.

To legalize prostitution would all but eliminate pimping and drug abusive prostitutes because there would be testing and regulations involved. Bureaucracy absorbs all the extra revenue and state and local governments become the pimps.

Another point about this one is that people with weird fetishes could go and pay for it instead of creeping out normal people or assaulting them. As you may have guessed, I'm for this one.

And yes of course I realize that prostitution is wrong and that it probably really shouldn't be legal, and that I am only justifying something that shouldn't be with a weak argument. And honestly if I was with anyone at the time of this writing I wouldn't even suggest it because I wouldn't be interested in it. But listen, I don't smoke, I don't drink alcohol, I don't use drugs, I don't gamble, hell, I don't even drink coffee. I need to indulge in something. Sex may as well be it, let me get high off my own endorphins. Please oh please oh please legalize this one! Okay, I'm done ranting, this is probably a bad idea…

Microloans

Listen, I've said it a million times if I've said it once, *people are stupid*. This is a fact of life. But it takes a special kind of bloodsucker to exploit people's idiocy for profit. And microloans are a good example. These check cashing and quick auto loan places are parasitic. They prey on people's desperation and lack of understanding of how these places work. That causes them to lose big when they can't pay up with staggering interest or seizure of property. I live in the Midwest and there are more of these check cashing places than there are gas stations out here. It's shameful. I don't think they should be allowed to take so much advantage of people's stupidity.

Conscription

Lots of countries have conscripted services, and we should be one of them. And I'm not talking about the draft. The draft is a desperation alternative the armed services uses in emergency shortages of men. I am talking proper conscription.

I think that everyone should join some branch of service at a certain age for the experience. Even an extreme short term service option may be possible, like say a year or 18 months. They can go to school while enlisted if they choose. Arrangements can be made with specialty colleges for highly intelligent students and athletes to accommodate them, like ROTC in high schools do.

Additionally, I think that juvenile offenders depending upon the nature of their crimes should be offered the option of armed service vs. actual jail time as an alternative. If the crime is not severe, but they are facing real time, offer them to trade their time for service to their country with the understanding that screwing up will put them back in the big house. The discipline and education offered by armed service could save their future.

And lastly, it could be an option for certain *qualifying* more "hard time" criminals who are already incarcerated for long terms to trade time with armed service during wartime. Let them earn their way back into society instead of bleeding it out with the enormous cost of housing long term inmates.

Co-Ed

Here is what you do. Get a massive group of teenagers who are going through puberty, give them sex-ed classes, and cram them together like sardines. Oh, wait, they already did that. It's called public school.

Co-Ed needs to stop. I know that this country likes to blow its own horn and scream about our great system of equality, but this doesn't work very well. We just pretend that it does because separating schools back into male and female categories would be amazingly expensive at this point. And since the government is well aware that public school is merely going through the motions, as far as educating the slobbering voting masses are concerned so it is not fit to sink real money into anything less than smokescreens.

Not that they are not wasting billions already. But if something worked, it would prove that nothing else does, and it would be embarrassing. Embarrassing means that someone would have to admit they were wrong, and we can't have that, now can we…

What Is It With...

There are some things that I just can't get past when I see it. I know that people are generally stupid and dirty, but there are certain things that just really make me wonder when I encounter them.

Bad Breath

What is it with people and their bad breath? Have we not long since entered a new age of hygiene? Never mind that so far as we know tooth brushing has been around since at least the Egyptians. I just don't get it when you encounter someone and their breath makes you take a step back.

Naturally, these tend to be the people with a lack of depth perception who have to step right up in your face to talk to you and make you feel like you are desperately holding back your lunch. What is wrong with these people? Brush your damn teeth!

And I swear little kids never brush. I have worked with many children and they come in fresh in the morning smelling of sweat and with breath like puppies. They are unwashed, unclean and with teeth un-brushed. Really now, get your kids in the habit of taking care of their personal hygiene while they are young and can develop the skill for life. Stop being cowardly about dealing with your kids. They fucking stink and it's your fault!

TB Tests

What is it with TB tests? Let me ask you this, who the fuck gets tuberculosis? As I have previously said, I have worked around a lot of children. This requires a lot of TB tests on my part by state government health agencies. And every time I step into another doorway of another agency that deals with kids, they want another TB test. I have had as many as ten in a six year period. That is bullshit.

I have never even heard of anyone with tuberculosis in my entire life. I have heard people coming from third world countries tell me that they have heard of people getting it where they came from, but not here. I could understand the widespread testing if there were like an epidemic or some shit, but never? And odds are that if I did get it I would catch it from someone who came from a poverty stricken country who recently entered the United States. They are the ones who need a fucking TB test, not me!

I am sick of getting a bubble test under my skin all the time. Watch, we will probably develop some weird mutant strain of tuberculosis because of the tests that can't be cured. Fuck that!

Daycare Neglect

What is with you parents who drop your kids at daycare? Not everyone, but enough that it is an issue. I have worked in and owned daycares. And I will tell you, as bad as some of these kids are to deal with, the parents are worse. The parents are the ones responsible for the little miscreants unruly behavior and bad habits either because they do not discipline their children, they do not pay attention to their children, or they enable their children's bad or odd behavior.

I cannot discourage a little boy from sucking his thumb if his mother does it. I cannot get a little girl to understand a good meal if her mother feeds her a bag of flaming-hot-fries and an orange soda pop for breakfast on the way to daycare. And I cannot get the child to be comfortable and settle down if the parent lingers because they are demanding some false expression of affection from a child who never receives any themselves so that they can show off in front of me.

And for the love of God, put some shoes on your kids. One of the biggest issues I have had is with parents trying to drop their kids with no shoes. I don't need to hear from some dad or mom that they have no shoes on because they couldn't get their two year old to cooperate. I'm sorry, who is in charge in your household? Try acting like you are and quit trying to argue with the kids to get what you need done. These children are not cognitively developed enough to debate you, why are you arguing with a two to five year old and expecting results? Why are you arguing with anyone under college age and expecting results?

Background People On TV

What is it with people in the background on live television broadcasts? Are we so desperate for attention as a species that we are willing to stand in groups of tens of thousands in the streets for hours in freezing sleet for the slim chance that a camera looking at someone who is actually interesting, (barely) might pan past you for a second so that you can wave at it? What is wrong with you?

Nobody is looking at you and nobody cares. You know who is looking? People like me who make fun of people like you for wasting so much of your time.

Modern Warfare

Newsflash, warfare is messy, violent, destructive and gruesome. So what is it with all these modern warfare tactics? And I don't mean new technology or training. I mean how the military has been pushed into being really weak with warfare because they are afraid of bad press.

The objective of war is to destroy an enemy, period. You destroy them, kill them and cripple them so that they cannot retaliate because of a lack of resources on every level. That is the intimidating factor that keeps a lot of countries from engaging in war in the first place, the fear that they might lose. If you do not look like the toughest kid on the block, someone is going to deck you.

Case in point, our modern military is moving away from the fighting man to the policeman/peace-coordinator/social worker. This is not soldering. And it has no place in warfare. While a soldier is sitting there bandaging scraped knees and giving away chocolate bars the enemy is burning us alive and putting our heads on pikes. They understand war, we no longer do. We are intimidated by bad press, and the press has no business in a warzone. The military needs to be left alone to do its job. War would go by a lot quicker if it were taken care of immediately, like in the first Gulf War. Make a big mess, sweep over it. The only problem then is that we didn't finish what we started. There was too much bad press.

And understand that what I say has nothing to do with the military branches themselves. I respect soldiers, I was set to enter the service myself before other obligations took that from me, and I regret it. Soldiers have their backs against the wall by people keeping them from doing the jobs they were sent out for, either because of greed or a false sense of acting civilized. A mistake we have been making since Vietnam.

Obsessive Dog Lovers

What is with you people who have a dog that you treat better than your child? If you even have a child, which is probably why you pamper the dog so badly. These animals are virtually toys to their owners who dress them and put jewelry on them and feed them with a spoon at the table. I knew a guy who had a dog that he used to paint her toenails, himself! But he wouldn't do it for his girlfriend? What kind of shit is that?

You people are obsessed and it is a form of abuse because none of it is natural to the dog's nature. You do not see wolves in the wild wearing umbrella hats and little raincoats. It doesn't happen. And it's not cute. It's sad. I feel sorry for these people because I imagine that they must be so terribly lonely. The dog is their child and their only friend in the world. That is sad. So much for the human condition…

Halloween

What is the problem with teenagers on Halloween? Is there no official cutoff age for trick-or-treating? There should be. I should not have what looks like the equivalent of a college basketball team knocking on my door asking for candy treats. What makes some six foot tall teenager who is like 17 years old think he is still eligible to go trick-or-treating? If they haven't grown out of adolescent mentality by this age, they never will. And what about these mothers who walk around on Halloween with newborns trying to trick-or-treat on their baby's behalf? Bullshit! Buy your own fucking candy with your food-stamp allowance! Leave the trick-or-treating to the little ones, older kids should stick to throwing eggs.

Multitasking

Ok, so what's with multitasking? Who told people they could to two or more things at once? They can't. They fuck one of them up, or barely scrape by with the two. What idiot thinks that they can keep getting away with driving while texting while drinking their coffee while reading the paper? Keep it up, paramedics are in high demand on our nation's highways. Multitasking is a lie. It is something that businesses convince you of so that they can eliminate jobs. Why have three people specializing in separate functions when they can force one person to do everything?

To do two things at once is to do neither (Publilius Syrus, an Iraqi enslaved by the Romans. Flourished first century BCE.) There is a lot to be said for this quote.

Whatever Happened To...

Ever notice how some things change? Did you ever sit there and wonder what the fuck happened to this or that because it used to be different when you were younger? Not better mind you, just different. Did you ever notice how much worse things seem with these new changes? What ever happened?

Table Manners

What happened to table manners? Where did they go? When did we go from looking like we are escaping the image of being human animals and backtracking into a more carnal state? I thought we were homo-sapiens; to watch some people eat, the term *homo-inferior* comes to mind.

I really do not want to see what is inside someone's mouth while they are chewing. I do not want to hear their gaping mouths mawing and slobbering food. I do not want to see food falling from someone's mouth while they chew or talk with their mouth full. It is disgusting. At least swallow what you are chewing before you start talking, I mean honestly.

And what happened to utensils? You have a fork and a spoon for a reason; you do not need to dig your fingers in your plate if you have utensils! Only traditionalist Muslims can get away with that. Use your utensils! Too many people are really gross when they eat.

Libraries

Whatever happened to the public library? I mean, they are still out there, I think that most cities have one, and most schools seem to have one, but what happened to them?

You know the library, the big building that is city property full of thousands of books and no-one reading. That place. The place where we used to go to read when we were kids, back when people could still read, you remember? Libraries are still public, and still loaded with books. And you see students there sometimes doing homework, and that's fine. It is still usually a fairly quiet place. But everyone else there is on a computer, usually playing games. This is not learning, it's not even useful. Any idiot kid can operate a mouse, and punch keys, even if they can't type or read. They can get online and fuck off the day playing games. I hate this.

I understand that libraries have introduced a large number of computers to maintain public interest, but the interest being generated defeats the purpose of drawing people in under such conditions. I am sure that research is being done by some with these systems, but more often than not it is just kids wasting time. Time is the one thing they can't get back, what the hell happened?

David Gudgeon

Spelling

So what happened with spelling? Stands to reason that if people can't read anymore, they can't fucking spell either. And here is another instance where computers heft some of the blame. You see, spell-check makes corrections for people. This was designed as a convenience, not a crutch. But as people are so damn lazy, it becomes a crutch. Now, if you are smart and work with word processing programs a lot like I do, you know that spell-check is often wrong and grammatically incorrect. But then, most people aren't that smart. And they accept whatever spell-check says and fuck up their work.

Here's a tip. If spell-check makes a correction, at least make yourself aware of the spelling change so that you can try to be mindful of it next time. Teach yourself to do it right.

Posture

I remember once upon a time when people used to stand and sit up straight. People used to actually tell you not to slouch because it made you look sloppy and stupid and it was bad for your body. Now it's popular to look like a bum so posture doesn't seem to matter anymore. Kids used to have to walk around with a book on their heads so they could learn better posture, now most kids can't even read a book. Welcome to the 21st century...

Being Kempt

There is nothing more aggravating to me than to see someone walking like a duck trying to keep their pants up because they have tethered them around their knees. Is there no-one left in this country under the age of twenty with their pants around their waist and with a belt? It sure seems that way sometimes. Who thinks this looks cute? How is this in any way practical? Are you kidding me? Pull up your fucking pants!

Manual Skills

Now, whatever happened to manual skills? People are getting worse when it comes to simple tasks. People have been learning to be too codependent on machines to do the work for them. People are getting to the point that they are unable to perform simple manual tasks.

People can't wash their clothes properly, they can't cook anymore, They couldn't start a natural fire in an emergency. These simple abilities that everyone could have done even a hundred years ago are slipping through our fingers. Look at knot tying. One of mans oldest tools is tying things together. Now having worked in a shoe store and from observation, I will tell you that people are losing their ability to even tie their shoes. I am amazed at how many people are walking around with their shoes tied incorrectly. They can't manage the simple knots necessary to keep their shoes on their feet. I know this from experience as I once worked in a shoe store. Many of the customers literally could not tie their shoes properly. What the fuck are we going to do as a species if this keeps up?

Language Skills

Well, what happened to language skills? We can't talk anymore? I swear I can hardly understand people anymore. Too many people talk like they have a mouth full of shit. I can't understand someone's words if they are chewing on them while they talk. We are losing the art of enunciation.

The words do not come out clearly enough for other people to understand. Even among groups that talk with the same backward ditchwater shit made up accents cannot understand each other. Everyone is talking twin-speak, and the twin is imaginary. No-one knows what you are saying dimwit! Fucking enunciate! Understand that you are not being understood. No matter how smart you are you will look like a damn moron if people cannot understand you.

And lay off the profanity. It's getting so people can't get a sentence out without cussing one out of every three of their words. I know even I am throwing some nasty words out in this format, but in real life, I hardly ever cuss. Something I taught myself because I am often around children, they may have a lot of bad habits, but they won't get them from me if I can help it.

Breastfeeding

Really now, what is up with this subject? For millions of years mammals, including humans have naturally breast fed their offspring, which unless you are very ill is the simplest most natural and most nutritious way to provide sustenance for the baby, (unless you are a koala, which in some cases is not much different than how many American babies are eating).

But now, since we have gotten so damn lazy it has been more of a convenience to feed a newborn from out of an industrially manufactured can, rather than offer ourselves up for our child. Too many women complain about how it is uncomfortable or inconvenient and pick up a can of formula instead. And I know I'm not a woman and I am sure I would be told that I don't understand what it is like to be one. No, I'm not, and there are some things that I probably wouldn't understand. But I know what is natural, and I know what works. And I also know that humans are weak and always looking for shortcuts to convenience themselves, even if it hurts or inconveniences someone else.

Ladies, at least try before you give up on breastfeeding, (and I don't mean once or twice, try giving it a week or so). Most women never even get that far. The lack of a bonding process is part of what is screwing all our kids up. Think about it. There is no bonding process in propping a bottle up in a crib.

Handwriting

When did we stop knowing how to write in cursive? It seems that every teenager I meet or work with anymore tells me that they do not know how to write in cursive, not even their own names. These kids sign things by printing their names, badly. They can't even fucking print words; I don't know how I should expect them to be able to write in cursive. But honestly and at the very least, they should have the ability to write their own signatures in cursive. It would be nice if they could at least sign a check, not that most of them could fill a check out. I've seen a lot of that too.

Work Ethics

Well, where are they? These work ethics? People used to give a shit about their jobs. Now all they seem to do is complain about them. Honestly, some of these jobs really do suck, but at least you are earning an honest living. I've done the cashier thing and the stocking shelves thing and the carrying trash thing, it sucks. I have also had some really good jobs, where everyone there made triple minimum wage or better with ten paid holidays, vacations, benefits, contests, freebies, paid sick days and on and on. And these people bitched. And I used to tell them, "you know, the supermarket is hiring, they need someone to push shopping carts for $6.50 an hour part time". They didn't like that. Okay, let's face it; most people do not like their jobs. We do not all get to be movie actors and football stars. But liking and not liking your job has nothing to do with how well you do your job or the fact that you need money.

You must understand that no matter what the job is or who the boss is, in reality you are working for yourself. You are your real boss and you contract your services to whomever it is you are employed by. To do shitty half-assed work and complain the whole way through is only a reflection on you. Be glad you are earning an honest dollar, even if it is not much money. I know what it is to scrape on with two jobs and still have nothing after the bills. I have lived off of noodles or cereal for every meal. I know what that is like. But don't take it out on your employer, even if they are pricks. They may deserve it but you will only hurt yourself. Besides, the truth is, if you really thought you could do better, you wouldn't be there.

Phone Etiquette

So, whatever happened to phone etiquette? Does anyone know how to use a phone anymore? You pick up, you dial, you talk, you say bye and hang up, simple, right? Not so simple. Now people have speaker phone so you have to listen to hazy background noise and try to decipher what the other person is saying. Or if they are not using the speaker, they have a stereo or a TV blasting in the background and you can't hear the conversation over the noise. It's fucking annoying.

Or here's my favorite, someone calls you and sort of talks with you but they don't really understand what you are talking about because they are not really paying attention to you on account of having a side conversation. If you are talking to someone else, why call me? Leave me the fuck alone! I don't like the phone anyway.

Animation

Whatever happened to decent animation? Cartoons have gotten so badly drawn I get a headache even looking at them. They are colored badly, articulated badly, they scroll badly. They look like shit. I know we have better skills than this, what the fuck? Take a look at the original Superman animated cartoons by Fleischer Studios made back in 1941. Brilliant work. Great color, great motion, good transfer, and an actual plot. This is how it used to be done. So what went wrong? Good got too expensive, that's what happened.

We are also substituting way too much animation with computer generated animation. It is fine for some things, but not everything. We are going to lose the skill of animation if we are not careful.

Dueling

And I ain't talkin' banjos! Yee-haw, what happened to dueling? You got two nitwits who can't resolve something, let em kill each other! Two less idiots to worry about! Yeah, I know, it's illegal to kill, and rightly so. You should not go around just murdering indiscriminately. It's counterproductive. But what's that got to do with dueling?

Okay, I'll compromise on this one. How about if every town has a town ring like they have a town hall, and when you have two morons who can't work their differences out, you let them fight it out. You can sell tickets, help the town's revenue. Of course they can only be matched up proper, we can't have a 20 year old professional boxer throwing down with an old man in a wheelchair. But match it up fair and let them sort it out. People would probably get along better if they did. Humans are naturally aggressive; let them take out their aggression in a proper forum instead of doing it in a way that will get them into trouble, (which is how it usually works out).

I think they should do this in schools where most kids are pretty evenly matched because they are all undeveloped. Let them scrap for a little bit, then make them shake hands and apologize. This is kind of how it used to be done, let the kids sort it out and watch closely so it can be controlled. Since they took these methods away, well, now look at the violence.

Pet Peeves

This may come as a surprise to you, but I actually have some pet peeves. Things that people do that I encounter that just burn my eggs when they happen. Things that make me wonder how the human race has managed to get this far. Things that make me wonder if Neanderthal man is actually extinct, or homo-sapiens cross bred with them somewhere down the line and the gene pops up in our offspring.

Anyway, here are a few little things that get under my skin...

Nail Biting

Oh my God, keep your fucking fingers out of your mouth! This enrages me! I hate seeing people biting their nails, sucking their fingers, picking their teeth and nibbling at their skin and cuticles. What are you like two years old! Knock it off! Keep your damn hands out of your mouth. It's unsanitary, unhealthy, unattractive and childish. Little kids suck their fingers; people who are like 35 shouldn't still be doing it!

Parking

Listen, I know that most people don't know how to drive properly, but can you at least master parking? It's two lines, you put your car in the middle. How hard is it? And if you screw up, you can pull out and go back in again. It's not like you only get one chance. Do it again! Get it right! What is wrong with people? If you can't center a car between two big yellow lines then you have no business driving at all.

Happy Birthday/Christmas/etc...

There is nothing more insulting to me, (in the moment) than a holiday or birthday card sent to me by the company I work for. These are thoughtless computer generated cards with printed signatures of people I do not even know, that I am sure do not know me. This is the companies attempt to pretend that they care about the employee without having to actually do anything for them in a way that costs the least. It is a thoughtless way to pretend that they are thinking about you. I wonder how many Jews, Hindus, Muslims and Buddhists got a company Christmas card this year?

Happy Birthday!!

While we are on the subject, I hate it when someone has a birthday and they announce it in a restaurant. There is nothing more annoying than watching these poor wait-staff droning to the restaurant company's version of "happy birthday" so that some customer can get a free brownie alamode. It's bad enough that the customer is probably lying to get a free desert, they have to torment a bunch of miserable customer abused low wage waiters and waitresses in the process.

Vaginal Spray

Vaginal spray, more commonly known as vaginal deodorant is, quite frankly, disgusting. I have news for you, we can smell it. We can all smell it and it mingles with the odor you are trying to cover up. And that makes it worse. It smells horrible, and it smells obvious. Spray is no substitute for hygiene. Please listen to me; there are times I have actually gagged at the smell.

Blocking The Aisle

If you are shopping, and you need something from the aisle and you think you are going to be a minute because you are too overwhelmed by the variety, pull the fuck over! Get your fucking cart out of the way so that other people can get by. Do you stop your car in the middle of the road and leave it when you need to go inside somewhere? Some of you probably do...

10 For 10

You see this in the supermarket sometimes. Ten for ten or five for five or something like it. The sale may be some item for like a dollar, but they say ten for ten because they know that blockheads will see it and think they need to get ten instead of just one or two. It is a marketing ploy, and unfortunately it works otherwise they wouldn't do it. It's insulting to my intelligence to have them try and force me to buy extra of some shit on sale.

Oversized Purses

Why the hell have some women got to wander around with a satchel that wouldn't qualify as carry-on luggage at the airport? How much shit do you need? I mean really. The funny thing is that when they dig into these things they can never find what they are looking for! They have everything but what they need, it only encourages them to pack even more shit for next time. Ridiculous! Get a normal sized bag; knock it off with the potato sack you're lugging around.

Wallets

And guys, please, buy a goddamn wallet! For every guy with a proper wallet, there is some chump that has a mountain of shit in their pockets walking around looking like *Dennis the Menace*. Marbles, sugar packets, jack-knife, yo-yo, 800 pennies, what the fuck? Grow up, buy a fucking wallet, they don't cost that much. Show some dignity; quit handing cashiers little balls of dollar bills to pay for shit. It's embarrassing.

Baggy Pants

News flash, there is a fashion accessory and it's called a belt. You do not actually need three pairs of boxers and two pairs of sweat pants to hold your jeans up. This makes you smell, (worse). Another news flash, jeans have sizes made to fit your waistline; you are not supposed to buy them ten sizes up so that they hang below your nuts. Wearing them so they actually fit your waist and putting on a belt will free up your hand that you have to use constantly to grip the front of your pants to keep them from falling all the way down. Then you have two hands to thrash in the air while you walk down the street talking to yourself and trying to look *hard*.

Grow up, little kids can't keep their pants up, are you a little kid? Back in the day, pants hanging off of your ass is how you advertised if you were gay and for sale, are you a gay prostitute? Couldn't be, most openly gay men dress better.

Flip-Flops

Flip-flops are footwear designed to be worn at the beach, at the pool or in a public shower. They are not made to be everyday footwear. I should not be seeing people wandering around in the streets with flip-flops on. I do not enjoy looking at your grubby dirty toes and badly placed tattoos.

And this goes double for slippers! Quit walking around in fucking slippers! They get filthy fast and they stink! Buy some real shoes!

Silverware

Huge common mistake that I hear all the time, silverware. Let's get this straight; silverware is not silverware unless it is made with actual silver. Everything else is flatware. Not silverware. Waiters/waitresses, you are not helping with this problem. I know you have the most thankless job in the world, but please call it flatware. This just drives me nuts...

Cashier Incentives

I hate it when you are in the checkout line and the cashier has to ask you a bunch of shit that has nothing to do with you. They want your phone number, they want to know if you want to make a donation, they want to know if you found everything you needed, they want to know if you need batteries or if you would like to try some shit candy bar that's on sale at the counter. NO! Fucking no! Leave me alone! If I wanted anything else, I would have asked you! Don't ask me! And no you can't have my phone number, what the fuck does the store need this for? Some survey? Bullshit! If it was a demographic survey they could ask for your zip-code. They don't need a phone number for that. Don't believe them! God this makes me mad. Just let me pay and get out, why is it so hard?

And of course you realize that they make the cashier do all that, so I do sympathize with the cashier to a point. But I also know that deep down inside they don't really give a shit if you need anything, they want you out as bad as you want to go.

Writing Checks

And while we are still in the market, what about these idiots who decide to write a check in line? As if the line isn't long enough and taking long enough already. Carry some cash shithead! Or use your debit card. Or maybe not, most of the people writing the checks are usually the ones who hold up the line because they can't remember their pin.

Rappers!

Everybody's a rapper, did you know that? Look, there goes one now! They're everywhere! Wandering aimlessly in the street rapping out loud indiscriminately to *themselves*. Don't you see them? Waving their arms in the air and yelling out loud, trying to look angry and holding their pants up. And if you make eye contact, they'll rap at you, like you are their private audience.

I tell you, you truly have to have an empty head for this sort of behavior to be part of your everyday lifestyle. Either that or they desperately crave attention.

Counting

Here is another item from the checkout line. Let me give you a scenario that often happens to me. I go to the store, check out, at the register, the cost is say, $3.13. Okay, so I give the cashier a ten and they screw up and give me change for a five and shut the draw. I bring the mistake to their attention, and here we go…

Now, it was $3.13, they thought it was a five, so I got $1.87 back, five to go, right? You would think it was that easy. Not for the rocket scientist I'm dealing with. This kid can't figure it out, so she calls the manager over who needs a calculator! Then they still can't manage the problem, and end up re-ringing the sale. You have got to be fucking kidding me… The manager of the store, and a girl in her early 20s, wearing a class ring no less, can't add $3.13 + $1.87 + $5.00 to get ten without a calculator, and still have to redo the sale. And this example actually happened! It's a sad world we're living in.

Roaches

Suffice it to say, I am not scared by bugs. But I do have a particular problem with cockroaches. I grew up with them in slums and it is amazing how easily people adapt to having to live with these creatures. Insects that by the way came originally from a tropical climate, and thrive in urban environments because of the people. If the people were not there, the roaches would all die. And I wish they would. I hate them because of my memories of them.

We as a species have a rather well rounded skill when it comes to eradicating other forms of life, but we can't get rid of the roaches. We kill everything we want, then can't get rid of what we don't. It's so human of us.

Daylight Savings

Daylight savings, why are we still doing this? What a colossal waste of time. Turn it forward, turn it back, <u>fuck</u> you. I don't want to change my clock. I don't want to drive to work in pitch black because it gets dark early. It's dark anyway, it's fucking winter moron! We're supposed to pretend it's sunny out by screwing with the clock? How does that help? Listen, World War Two is over. We don't do blackout time anymore. Let this shit go. And don't give me any crap about farmers needing it either, they are going to get up with the sun no matter what time it is, they're farmers!

Clean Your Plate

Okay, so I'm sitting in a sub-shop, there is a couple sitting across from me; he gets this huge sandwich with chips and a drink. He eats half, some of the chips, drinks his drink, and throws the other half in the trash on the way out. Fucking bastard! How dare he! People all over the world are starving to death, and this guy is throwing the equivalent of an entire meal in the garbage. My God…

Especially being someone who grew up with a firsthand knowledge of hunger, this makes me angry. He could have at least taken a doggie bag. Bring your shit home. You are too important for leftovers? It must be nice. It must be nice to be so goddamn important that you can throw food away arbitrarily. Even at home, when I have stuff I know I'm not going to eat, I put it out for the local wildlife to finish off. It came from nature; I gave it back to nature when I couldn't use it. Fair is fair. Throwing away good food is not fair. It's appalling.

I see a lot of this in buffet restaurants too. People pile their plate's way up, then can't finish it. The food has to be disposed of because of health codes. Why jam the plate up? The food isn't going anywhere, it's a fucking buffet. They are bringing more. But people like to take more than they need, then dispose of it. I guess it makes them feel important. People are pigs.

The Post Office

I have nothing against the Post Office. For the most part, they do a great job. What irks me is the people who go in the Post Office. You know who I mean, these people who walk in and have no clue why they are there. Why are they there? Clue one, it's a Post Office! You mail shit! What is wrong with you people?

I stand in line for what seems like hours while one troglodyte after another steps up to the counter with a pile of shit and no box, needs help to select a box, needs help with the address, needs help with the labels, and on and on and on. "*What type of shipping service do you need maam*"? "*Gee I didn't think of that, what do you think I should do*"? Don't you know? Figure it out! Why does the clerk have to tell you what to do with your shit? How stupid is this? And the stamps, "*what kind do you have, can you show them all to me, which ones do you think I should get*"? Make a decision on your own, shit!

And these clerks are the most patient people on Earth. They smile and go on. Postal customers are mindless. If I had to deal with that all day every day, I'd go Postal!

Restrooms

Or more precisely, <u>public</u> <u>restrooms</u>. I don't like restrooms anyway. But there is a certain etiquette to them which should be observed, and is not. Now, I can't tell you very much about what goes on in the ladies room, but in the men's room there are some issues. It is just too casual for my taste. I am not in there to carry on a conversation. Leave me the fuck alone. I am disposing of bodily waste. I don't want an audience, and I don't need any help. Fuck off! Why would you look through the crack in the door to see if you recognize anyone and then stand there and strike up a conversation? I want some privacy. Leave me alone. When you are at a urinal, (and I really hate these things) don't get into the one right next to me and look at me and talk! Look at the wall and don't talk to me! Better yet, go three more down and stare at that wall, why are you so close? Get away from me!

And some of these restrooms are so dirty that I feel I am better off if I don't wash my hands. I don't want to touch anything. It's the one scenario where I feel a little germaphobic. A really nasty restroom will put me in that kind of neurotic mood.

Whining

For me, this is a very serious problem. I cannot stand whiners. This is something that children do, but unfortunately, many children do not grow out of the habit. They become teenage whiners, and then adult whiners, which is even worse. It is a horrible thing to deal with someone who is in their twenties or thirties that behaves like someone that is eight years old. When you are young, the squeaky wheel gets the oil, when you are older, the squeaky wheel gets replaced. These people lose jobs, friends, and the respect of peers and relatives, and never understand what the problem is. They just whine about how things aren't fair and people don't treat them fair and how life isn't fair. Well, life isn't fair, get over it. And shut the fuck up, it's not fair for anyone else either, but they cope with it and accept it and work through it, they don't whine and snivel like a little fucking kid. **Shut up!** Nobody wants to hear your whiny shit.

What's In A Name?

I have a pretty average name, David. Very simple, right? Not Dave, not D, David. If I wanted to be called anything else, I would say so. I would say, "Just call me Dave". But I don't, I like David. But people take it upon themselves to rename you. If your name is Richard, they call you Dick. If you are William, they call you Bill. Hey, show some respect. If the person wants to be called by a nickname, they will tell you. This irritates the hell out of me.

Conversation

Did you ever have someone standing around talking to you and you really wanted to get away from them? You try to be nice and you make excuses and you motion that you are leaving, and they just keep on yammering. Can't some people take a fucking hint? Back off, get lost! Learn some social cues. Reading body language is getting to be another lost art. And it doesn't just irritate me when it's me that's being bothered. I see this a lot with women and there is some creepy idiot trying to chat her up and she obviously doesn't want shit to do with him and he won't go away and keeps trying to talk his game. *Stupid mother fuckers*. And we wonder why women think men are thick headed. Too many of them can't take a hint!

Text Messaging

Sending a text message on your cell-phone is fine. It's convenient, it's easy. Or it should be. But some of these phones seem to want to predict your sentence based on what you typed last time and fill in words as you go. Then you are half way through typing and you have sentences that make no sense because there are words that shouldn't be there. Since when do I need a machine to finish my sentences? What the hell kind of crap is that? Are we getting that lazy? We probably are. It's pathetic. Is there a way to turn this feature off? Maybe I should read the manual sometime, but you see, I actually use my phone for phone calls, and little else.

Chewing

Call me crazy, but listening to people chew drives me nuts. I can't stand to hear people chewing. You put something in your mouth, you close your mouth, and you chew. That is how it's done. But a lot of people don't seem to be able to manage the second step. They chew with their mouths open and I have to listen to them gnashing their food. It's disgusting. Are we losing our ability to breathe through our noses? Or is breathing through the nose and chewing at the same time too much of a task for the average genetically defective human?

Phone Messages

Another simple task. You call someone, they don't answer, you get a voicemail, you leave a message. Did you get that last part? <u>You</u> <u>leave</u> <u>a</u> <u>message</u>! If you had something important enough that you were going to call someone in the first place, why hang up on the voicemail? Don't call me if it's not important! Leave a message. I won't answer your call, but I won't know why you called if you don't leave a message. I probably won't call you back, but at least I will know *why* you called.

On Hold

Okay, you call a doctor's office, they are very busy, they put you on hold, and you wait. I'm cool with this. It's business. But why must you call me and then put me on hold? Who calls somebody and puts them on hold? I mean shit! It's like, "*I called you but now my interest is waning because you're suddenly not that important anymore, let me put you on hold real quick, kay*"? If anyone ever does that to you, hang the fuck up…

The Homeless

Or more to the point, people trying to help the homeless. There are always people trying to help someone, and not knowing how. The homeless is a great example of this. When I was in Boston, (Boston had a large homeless population when I was there) I was always seeing blanket drives. Now think about this really hard, where is a homeless person going to keep a fucking blanket? Is he going to spread it over his queen sized bed in the duplex he built out of refrigerator boxes? Get real. They are called *homeless* for a reason. They have no home. If they have no home, they have no-place to keep their shit. All their things must be things that they can carry with them. A blanket does not fit these criteria.

A blanket gets in the way, and will be thrown away by the person you are trying to help. Donate something that the homeless can use right away that can be carried easily. Underwear, socks, toothbrushes, glasses, (the kind that go on your face). Use some common sense, I know people are stupid, but come on…

Nails

I do not like long nails, fingers or toes. Especially toes, especially on a guy. Cut your nails! You are not the emperor of the Ming Dynasty, you are a bum who is lazy and trying to look cute, cut your fucking nails! They are dirty and they are gross!

And this goes for women too. I don't understand this fetish about long nails being sexy or attractive. I don't get it. I think it's terribly unattractive and obtrusive. And artificial nails on a woman are like a comb-over on a man, it just doesn't look right. And that goes double for toenails! Nails should be short.

I No Understand

I hate it when people live in a country for years and still don't know the language farther than what it takes to tell you that they don't understand the language. If you are traveling, it is helpful to learn some phrases to get by. If you are moving to a country permanently, then you learn the language. Not in America! NO! You come here, we learn your language! Shit, we accommodate everybody! Come on in!

But you know even worse than this is when you are sure that they understand you but they act like they don't because they don't want to deal with you. I had a lot of trouble like this when I used to work in convenience stores when I was younger. You would have a couple of women wandering around and you can hear them talking and you know what they are saying because it is ENGLISH. And their rotten kids eat some candy bars in the corner, (fucking thieves) and you try to tell them that their kids ate some shit and that you expect them to pay for the little troll's micro-crime, and suddenly, all you get is confused looking smiles and nods. Bullshit! Lying sack of shit! You understand me! Own up for your spoiled tramp child!

Damn I hate that…

Pacifiers

I do not like pacifiers. Never did. I never used them with my kids, and I never had a problem. They never developed an oral fixation, and they never put their fingers and hands and pencils and anything else that would fit into their mouths. In fact, I hate pacifiers.

Pacifiers are not for the children, they are for the parents. They are a quick fix shut up device that parents use, (abuse) on their children when they don't want to deal with them. If you paid attention to your child and were in tune with them, you wouldn't need a pacifier.

And don't give me any crap about teething. That is not what it is for. A pacifier starts off as a method of fooling the baby into thinking it is feeding, and then it becomes a habit through continued use, thus addicting the child to the sucking action itself instead of using the sucking in its natural function. That is how you end up with five and six year olds who still walk around with a fucking binky! And that is why so many much older children, (and adults even) have a constant desire to stick something in their mouths.

And while we are on the subject, get those older kids out of the strollers and make them walk. I hate seeing a six year old in a stroller. Unless there is something wrong with the kid or the parent physically, there is no excuse. Either the parents are lazy, or the child was never disciplined and the parents can't control it. Both are bad. Make the kid walk.

Shop Talk

If I am at work, why would I want to talk about work? I'm already there; I already know what's been happening. Why tell me about it? I don't want to talk about work. I don't even want to be at work, so why prattle on about something I don't want to be doing? It's either shop talk or it's sports talk. I don't want to talk about sports either. I don't want to talk about other people's lives. I want to talk about my life, and not with you. You are at work and I don't want to be here. Stop talking to me!

Boy Or Girl?

I know that children seem asexual; they are all essentially shaped the same. But people are so conditioned towards the female stereotype that every baby they see is automatically a female at a first glance. You could have a baby boy in a black stroller in a completely blue outfit with "*I'm a boy*" written across his chest, and people will come up to you and ask you how old your daughter is. People are so stupid about this. They always guess female first because the feminine is associated more closely with babies. I mean certainly, women give birth, and women are biologically designed for children. But that does not automatically make every baby you see female. That is just really ignorant. Maybe they should make more boy baby dolls. In a few generations the confusion may balance out a little bit.

Handwriting

No, the other kind of handwriting. I'm talking about when some moron has such little confidence in their memory and are so disorganized that they have to write literally everything on their damn hand or arm. I can understand if you are really in a pinch and you are left with no choice, but I have seen people who write absolutely everything on their damn hands. Snap out of it and buy a notebook!

Water Water Everywhere

Water has been around longer than we have. It is the essential building block that is infused in every life form that we know of on this planet. The average person needs to consume half a gallon of water daily, and an athletic person two to three times this much. So why the hell is it that people won't drink it anymore? Suddenly humans are too damn good for water. They don't want it. "*Water? I'm not drinking that!*" What the hell's wrong with it? People would rather have drinks made with corn syrup or beer instead. Then they want to complain about being sluggish and fat. Serves them right…

Because Because Because

If you are asked a question, give an answer. If it is a simple question, give a simple answer. If a grocery clerk says, "paper or plastic" you answer, paper or plastic. It's that easy. You do not have to give a long drawn out explanation as to why you are making the decision you are making. No-one gives a shit. Just say what you want and go on. If the cashier asks you're your phone number and you don't want to give it, you say no. You don't have to write an essay describing why. You are dragging out the situation needlessly and making people want to choke you. Quit over explaining shit. The line at the market is long enough without your dumb ass grid-locking it.

Hitting The Head

Here is an area that is really starting to get on my nerves recently. Fully automated restrooms. They are popping up everywhere now. Auto flush toilets, auto react faucets, auto soap dispensing, auto towel dispensers and auto dryers, all with motion sensors for our convenience because humans are suddenly so paranoid about germs. Well okay germaphobes, wrap yourself around this, what are you going to do if you are on a toilet at the mall and there is a power failure? I seriously doubt the backup power supplying the emergency lights is going to flush your floater or wash your hands for you.

Litterbugs

I hate it when I'm driving and some asshole throws something out of the window from the car in front of me. You have to wonder what kind of inconsiderate prick it takes to wad up their trash and just drop it wherever the hell they happen to be, even at 70mph on the highway. Too good to junk up their own stuff, so they have to leave it on everyone else. Just throw it anywhere. Smokers are the worst with this. They are too accustomed to throwing things around because they drop cigarette butts everywhere they go. I remember working at convenience stores when I was younger and every person who bought a pack of cigarettes did the same lousy thing each time. They peel the cellophane off of the box, pull the foil out, roll them into a ball and drop them on the counter right in front of me. Fucking assholes. And you all wonder why cashiers look like they are pissed off all the time...

Please Pass The Salad

Okay, so there is really nothing wrong with salad all by itself. I eat salad, lots of people do, and that's fine. But I am a vegetarian. And I am the type of vegetarian that does not eat red meat or poultry. Now, many people are not accommodating to vegetarians, mostly because they don't understand it. And I am talking about going to a party or function or company picnic and being completely left out because even the green beans and mashed potatoes have bacon in them. Then you have to look like a stuck up ass trying to explain why you don't want a greasy grilled burger. You say you don't want red meat, they offer you pork. You say you don't eat poultry, they offer you turkey. This is because most people are stupid and they don't understand you. But what really irritates me is when you say you are vegetarian there is always some schmuck who says, *"well there's salad"*. Fuck you salad! If I ate nothing but lettuce and ranch dressing I would starve to death! Fucking salad, give me a break.

Bees

People, quit being stupid when it comes to bumblebees. Leave the bees alone. For the most part, they are harmless and not interested in you at all. People see these creatures and behave like someone is doing a drive-by shooting, screaming and waving their arms and running around. Besides, considering that a bee cruses at about 10mph, you wouldn't get far if it were really after you. And many bee varieties do not even have a stinger, shows what you know about bees. They are probably the most useful insects on

Earth, and I'm not talking about honey either. They are responsible for a huge portion of the cross pollination needed to sustain the regeneration of plant life. And what do we do? Kill them. How human.

Prayer

I am not saying that there is anything specifically wrong with prayer, but have you ever really thought about what it is that people pray about and for? Because quite frankly, most prayer is very selfish. First of all, it was my understanding that we are supposed to be minding ourselves and finding our own way. But it seems to me that many people instead of working out their own solutions like they are supposed to, and even expected to, they are begging for some cosmic entity to manage the problems for them. This is selfish and this is lazy. I could understand a prayer like, *"Aunt Suzie is dying of cancer, I pray she goes painlessly"*. That's not selfish. *"Lord, let me win the lottery"*, or *"God I want you to help me come in first in this race today"* that is selfish. Pick your own numbers and run your own race.

I Was First

I hate when people make a big deal about someone being first in something because of their color or gender. Really now, I do get it. It is supposed to represent the tolerance of the masses that someone outside of a particular cultures norm from a historical perspective gets to do something that people in their category had not previously done. I get it. But here is my problem...

Until we get to a point that someone of a different color or a different gender doing something is no big deal, then there is no true accomplishment. And this does not just go for the Western World. This is everywhere, every country. No population of any country wants to see what they consider an outsider or someone different doing anything important in their territory. People are afraid of change. They like sameness because it is predictable. They also do not like to feel as if they are being forced out. So I hate being spoon fed differences to show change. People will never change. They will always look for the bases differences because they are ignorant and afraid.

Here is an example. A religious example, (I know, but bear with me). I have heard the argument about the color of Jesus. Was he black, or was he white? I can answer that question for you. He was neither, he was Jewish. Not black, and not white. <u>Something else</u>. The reason he was originally depicted as white was because white people were doing the worshiping. Then when black people were doing the worshiping, they wanted him black. And there you are, man once again creating God in his image, instead of the other way around.

Listen, we all came from the original person model. As I described it earlier, the *proto-human*. Whoever he was and whatever his color or physical dimensions, we do not know. But we need to get back to the basics if we are to survive. This is why I like to see biracial children, of any mixed nationalities. Because they are not us, they are different. They have an opportunity to be better, if we will let them. They don't have to be petty and squabble about color differences like everyone else, because they can blend together. Then, they will only have to fight about religion and cultural differences.

Well, one out of three is a start…

Wouldn't It Be Fun?

There are some things I have always wanted to do just to be an ass. I wonder if I am the only one who thinks that these things would be fun. Here is a sample list of what I am talking about.

- When filling out a job application and it asks about sex, instead of putting male or female, write *yes please* in the box.
- On the same application under who to call in an emergency, write *call a doctor.*
- On any document that asks for your nationality, check the box that says other, and write some made up word no-one ever heard of before on the line.
- Save up all your junk-mail for an entire year and burn it in the fireplace.
- When someone asks you what you think of their new baby, and it is particularly ugly, tell the truth! In fact, ask them why they even attempted it considering how ugly they are!
- Mail someone a package full of gelatin.

- Glue the lids to someone's garbage cans shut.
- Fill someone's trunk with dildos.
- Freeze those little octopus that come in a can inside ice-cubes for your next party and act like you don't notice anything wrong with it.
- Tell your manager that the reason you left your previous job is because you punched out your old manager.
- Get a big muscular guy to walk around in the subway wearing a really nice three piece suit and a pair of really tall stripper's stilettos. Follow him around and photograph people's reactions.
- Put on torn clothing and splatter yourself with fake blood. Then run through the street screaming *"they stole my kidney"*!
- The next time the company you work for or your kids school wants to railroad you into a bake sale, bake something that tastes really awful on purpose. Set it out anonymously and stand somewhere you can watch people's reactions when they taste it.
- (Guys only). Next time you are on a blind date, wear a really big cowboy hat, boots, and a dress shirt with the sleeves torn off. Instead of flowers, give her a singing fish plaque. Intermittently in conversation yell at the top of your lungs, *"yee-haw! That's just like a cowboy!"* Tell her you enjoy running down traffic cones in your truck and your hobbies include making your own jerky out of road-kills you find. At dinner, bury your food in ketchup. When your friend who fixed up the date asks you what the hell happened, deny everything.

- (Girls Only). If you are on a blind date, test your mans courage. Walk up to some monstrous looking thug in a bar, (you know, the four hundred pound body builder with the swastika tattoo on his forehead opening his beer with his teeth). Tell him that your boyfriend noticed how he keeps staring and that he said he was about to "*whup some Nazi redneck ass*". As soon as you walk away, call the cops and the paramedics, by the time they get there, it should be over.

People Are

What are people? I mean, aside from physiologically, what makes people what they are? Well, I can answer that question, but you are not going to like it. If you wanted to hear about the niceties of humanity, you have the wrong damn book, something you should have figured out a few chapters back.

Everybody it seems has a bit of, if not all of the ingredients from this chapter stewing in their individual soup of life, including myself. Not everything applies to everyone, but there is enough rotten behavior to go around. Perhaps by some miracle someone will read this and find some truth in it, altering their perceptions of themselves, making them a better person. Or maybe not, but either way, here we go…

- **Indecisive**: People have become nearly incapable of making up their damn minds about anything. If you give anyone more than one choice, they are completely lost. Sometimes they are lost with only one choice. Don't believe me? Just watch someone trying to order off of a dinner menu. For some people, this is like a surgeon trying to pick the right scalpel in the middle of an operation when the one they need is not available. Fucking brain surgery to choose between broccoli or rice as a side dish. Pathetic. This is how humans have learned to avoid taking responsibility. If they make no decisions, then they are responsible for nothing. But being devoid of choices by allowing others to decide for you is a terrible crippling weakness. If you cannot make up your mind, someone will do it for you. People like this because they do not have to think. But it is not a good thing.

- **Undignified**: People are not only lazy slobs, but they get off on showing everyone just how slovenly and nasty they can be. Many people have given up on themselves so completely that they do not even attempt to even *pretend* to be anything more than wallowing pigs.
- **Easily Fooled**: People are fucking pushovers. They will believe almost anything if it is presented the right way, and sometimes if it's not. The most obvious fucking bullshit becomes gospel if the person telling it sounds convincing. People are amazingly soft in the head.
- **Inconsiderate**: People are assholes. They don't stop to think about how what they do affects others. Stopping to think about the aftereffects of their actions might inconvenience them from what they want. So why worry about the collateral damage?
- **Indecent**: People like to act nasty. They do nasty things and try to pretend that they don't because they are worried about what other

indecent people might think about them. Like somehow, they are just that much more lewd than the next guy, so best not to draw attention to oneself.

- **Sloppy**: People leave a trail of mess everywhere they go like great ugly slugs dragging a slime trail behind them. They will drop what they have wherever they are with no regard whatsoever. People will throw things and stack things and pile things and wonder what happened to all the space. Then they leave it behind and start all over to contaminate a new space.

- **In Denial**: Most people are actually aware that they are all fucked up, but nobody has the balls to admit it. They refuse to admit that they have problems; it's everyone else who has the problems! People will swear on their lives that there is nothing wrong, and if the problem is too obvious, well then they have it under control and can stop anytime!

- **Mentally Ill**: Just about everybody has something wrong with their minds. Not necessarily some sort of actual brain damage or physical brain deformity, but something wrong with the actual function that is linked to some personal or emotional issue. If you don't think so, then re-read the previous item.

- **Unskilled**: People can't do shit anymore. Humans used to be well versed in a wide variety of manual skills that people just can't seem to do anymore. I don't remember the last time I met someone who could actually cook or sew or do any basic shit that used to be so common place that it was no big deal even fifty years ago. What happened to our skills?

- **Violent**: People like to hurt things and they like to fight. They like to yell at other people and threaten them, and they like to destroy property. When they are not fighting or causing harm or destroying something, they are watching someone else do it. Then they want to pretend like they are not because they are worried about what other people might think so they pretend to be different so that they can appear civilized.

- **Gossips**: People like to run their mouths about other people's business. They want to pry into things that they have nothing to do with, knowing full well that their big mouths are making things worse. They talk about things they don't understand and condemn people for actions that often pale in comparison to the secrets that the gossipers are keeping. It makes people feel big to flap their gums about how much lower other people seem.

- **Untalented**: People no longer possess interesting skills. Once upon a time everybody could sing and dance and juggle and play games and instruments and perform all sorts of tricks. But not anymore. Nowadays people use trivia as a skill marker. That is the ability to know about other people who are interesting in detail, because you are not.

- **Uninteresting**: Saw this one coming, didn't you? People are fucking dull. Dull, dull, dull, and dull! The world is a big kitchen drawer full of old knives and scissors. Rusty and dull.

Even the people who seem interesting turn out to be tedious when you actually talk to them. What happened to all the entertaining people? Are they all dead? Or did we kill them all with boredom?

- **Weak**: Human beings are weak willed creatures. People will almost always fold and throw in the cards at the first sign of difficulty or hardship. They would rather give in than fight if the fight has to come to them. It is the rare individual anymore who will tough life out to reap the rewards. What a bunch of wimpy milk-toast motherfuckers we have become.

- **Feeble**: People are not limited to being weak willed, they are frail of body as well as spirit. Staying strong with simple things like healthy diet and exercise is far too difficult for the average person. Better to just be a worm wriggling in pain under the load of your own body weight and mask the discomfort with pills.

- **Unimaginative**: It is the rare individual with true imagination. People used to have it, but it is being bred out of us by the public school system. They prefer to make children use their imagination in other ways, like pretending that they will all grow up to be president. That is using imagination to pretend your way through life, and it is not the same as being imaginative. Being imaginative creates art and develops science; using imagination creates fucking daydreamers who never finish anything.

- **Jealous**: People are defiantly jealous. If someone has something that another person doesn't they are hated for it. It doesn't matter how they got it, or how hard they worked to earn it. People will automatically hate them for it. The reason being that they are too weak willed to push themselves hard enough to earn it for themselves, so they just want it given to them instead. And then have the nerve to be angry with someone else for being successful. That is the real reason that so many people whine about hating the rich.

- **Vulgar**: People like to do nasty things on purpose. They act gross and crass because they think they are being funny or because they want attention and don't care how they get it. Either that or they are so badly bred or so badly raised that they don't realize how raunchy their behavior is.

- **Cheats**: Humans like to rip each other off. People are always sniffing out the low road if it will benefit them without having to work at it. So if the opportunity turns up to rip someone off, your average person is likely to snap that opportunity right up. This is the reason why it is that when I worked as a cashier, even in different places, they allowed for a certain amount to be missing from the register daily. They anticipated that most people would not return extra change if it were given them by mistake. And the drawer was almost always short.

- **Thieves**: People will steal anything that is not nailed down if given half the chance. People are experts at convincing themselves that they deserve something that isn't theirs, so they compensate by taking it. Why do you think that everything is so goddamned expensive? It sure isn't because of high quality. It's because of shoplifting, and it's because of the high cost of security and surveillance equipment. If your local department store didn't need 300 cameras and its own security force, the prices might be a little lower.

- **Loud**: Humans are fucking loud. They make so much goddamn noise I'm surprised that we are not all deaf by the time we are thirty. We are forever making a shit load of noise, then trying to talk over it instead of turning everything down to a dull roar. And people talk so loud anyways. It is a byproduct of poor education and bad upbringing. When you are not smart and you know it, and when you grow up being ignored, then the only way to be noticed is to be louder than everyone else. So you keep raising your voice until it gets stuck there.

- **Parrots**: People like to repeat themselves. If they say something that sounds clever or they get a good reaction, (like laughter for example) from something they said they will say it over and over again trying to duplicate the response. This kind of behavior shows a lack of intelligence and a lack of confidence.

- **Unhealthy**: People do not take good care of themselves, physically or emotionally. They do not eat as they should and they do not exercise often enough, if at all. They indulge in risky behavior and bad habits that further wear down and even poison their bodies. Their bodies literally fall apart as they age because of this lazy behavior, and then have the nerve to complain about it as if it were someone else's fault and or responsibility. Then rather than correct the problem, they take pills to mask the symptoms or hide the pain. People are fully aware of what they should be doing, but few ever do it.

- **Un-nurturing**: Humans are losing their ability to take care of their young. They do not want the responsibility, and expect someone else to do it for them. Schools, government agencies, grandparents, (who produced the parents who are shirking their responsibilities in the first place) all have no business raising children. The people directly accountable for creating the children are responsible. But they do not want the burden, so they put it off on someone else, or neglect their duties. Either because they never learned how to nurture, or because they are irresponsible. This only compounds the problem by creating generation after generation of defective parents. Raising and caring for a child is becoming another lost art.

- **Stubborn**: People can be really fucking hard headed, trust me on this one, I am one of the hardest headed people you may ever meet. But the problem is that this tenacity is misused. Instead of flaring up that backbone for a good cause or for self improvement or self defense, or to change something that is out of order, humans will be hardheaded over stupid things that make no sense or are none of their damn business.

- **Depth Perception Deficient**: People lack depth perception. They always seem to be either too close or too far away from what they are doing or whom they are talking to. Because of this misunderstanding of other peoples safe zones, we are always in each other's way. Try to be at arm's length, is it that hard? You should not be close enough to smell someone's breath unless you intend to kiss them.

- **Dirty**: Lots of people are generally not very clean. The human body becomes fouled very quickly through the expulsion of waste by various means including sweat and shedding of skin. It is not really that much effort to maintenance the human body by keeping it clean, inside and out. But too many people's idea of controlling the odors associated with this think that a mess load of perfume, cologne, or deodorant will solve the problem. It does not. It makes it worse. The human stench mixed with chemicals is not pleasant by any means. Wash your body, brush your teeth, change your clothes, quit being nasty.

- **Quarrelsome**: People like to get into mess with other people. They shoot off their mouths without any means to back up what they say either factually or physically if it comes to it. They like to make a big primitive display of their trashy unjustified bravado to show off for people who could give a shit outside of being entertained by watching a fight.

- **Provoking**: People also like to try and provoke other people into deliberate confrontations so that they can act like they were attacked and are completely innocent. These are people who want an altercation with someone, but know that they are wrong for their actions and try to hide this fact by goading someone else into a confrontation. Then they can pretend to be innocent and save face with the drooling audience.

- **Instigators**: People are also pretty good at heating up other people to go after each other. Humans like conflict, and all the better if it is someone else in conflict so you can sit back and enjoy the show. Furthermore, it gives some people an illusion of power if they think they are controlling someone by manipulating their actions or emotions.

- **Judgmental**: Humans are very good for making split decisions about people based on appearance, accent, clothing style, pitch of voice or anything else that seems different. Sometimes this is a good instinct. Sometimes you can go with your gut and you are right about someone and you make the right choices based on your impression. The trick here is not to actually *judge* someone. To judge someone outright is also to condemn them, and this is where people falter.

- **Habit Forming**: People fall into patterns of behavior that are not always, (mostly not) good for them. They drink alcohol, smoke cigarettes, use drugs recreationally, gamble, pick their nose, and do a hundred other things that they shouldn't. They are fully aware of the physical, emotional, and financial damage that it does both to themselves and the people around them, and assume no responsibility unless forced to. The real weakness here is that any habit can be exchanged for another because the human condition allows for and often requires a compulsive behavior. This is the reason why it is that so many people who give up some habit, form another almost immediately. You quit smoking, you start eating, you get your stomach stapled to quit eating, you become a sex addict and so on. But if you are smart, you can select a habit, a useful one, if you are smart.

- **Pharmaceutical Junkies**: People due to their weak dispositions will take pills for just about anything no matter how bad the side effects are. Swallowing a pill is the easy way out to avoid doing what they should, (diet and exercise vs. a diet pill for example). If it requires effort and discipline but there is a pill that does almost the same thing even though the side effect will require you to take three more pills to alleviate the discomfort of the first, then people will take the pills rather than change their diet or their bad habits.

- **Fixated With Holes**: Humans are not so far out of the trees that they can leave a hole alone for long. Humans are fixated with them. If there is a hole, they will stick something in it. Usually their fingers, and usually their own holes. People are constantly digging in their ears, mouths, noses, bellybuttons, asses and everywhere else that a finger may fit. Then they pretend that they are not digging and try to disguise the behavior. People will even interfere with holes that are too small for fingers to mess with, like pores. And if they can't mess with their own holes, they are playing with someone else's.

- **Dishonest**: People are not honest if they can help it. People act like they want to be honest, but it mostly doesn't work out that way. People will lie about absolutely anything no matter how stupid and pointless it is if they think it will save their asses or make them look better. The problem is that people are also mostly very bad at lying, and are easily seen through by others. Probably because other people lie so much, they recognize the lying routine too easily. Kind of makes you wonder why anyone bothers to lie.

- **Loving The Lie**: People love to be lied to. They want to believe things that are not because the reality of what is can be humbling and frightening. People would rather accept a very questionable falsehood than face reality and acknowledge the truth. People accept lies out of fear. They fear what others may think, and they fear what they may think and the repercussions of their thoughts. Independent thought can be a dangerous thing. Believing the lies can protect one from the persecution of the ignorant and the oppressors. Believing the lies can suppress fear, for a time…

- **Untrustworthy**: People cannot be trusted. If you can trust the average person to do anything, it will be to do the exact opposite of what they say that they are going to do. They are too worried about satisfying their own agenda to worry about doing right by someone else.

- **Poorly Educated**: People are not well read. They never have been and they are not now. It is only the elite who are very well educated. And mostly, this is the fault of the individual. People are not interested in the amount of hard effort involved in grinding away with their cognition, they would rather let the gears rust. Sitting back and being dumb is easy, and humans like easy. Learning is hard, fuck hard! That is why geniuses are in such short supply. And don't give me that crap about the availability of education. Some of the most impressive geniuses in history were mostly if not completely *self taught!*

- **Not Civilized**: Human beings are not well civilized, never have been. But because people are so overly conscious of what they think other people think of them, they like to pretend that they are. Then if they happen to live in a society that is a little better off than their neighbor, it gives them an excuse to look down their noses at their neighbor, judge them, and get all up in their business. The notion of civility is an excuse for indulging a superiority complex. If people were really civilized, they would understand other people's differences, even if the subjects were incredibly primitive by nature. A civilized person would mind their fucking business instead of trying to forcibly transpose their ideals onto another culture. This is only an attempt at self justification. "*I know I'm better if I can convince another person that I am well enough to copy me*". That's bullshit!

- **Pretenders**: People like to pretend that they are more than they are. People are not satisfied with who and what they are, but rather than seeing the problem for what it is and seeking to improve themselves they lie about themselves instead. It seems that it is much easier to lie than it is to do a little work that may help to develop an individual's skills, intelligence or body. Lying is so much easier, even if the lie is so painfully obvious that no-one believes it.

- **Conceited**: Humans all have a common problem, it is called *center of the universe complex*. Every single person thinks that they are the most important thing in the whole world. No matter how stupid or worthless they know themselves to be, they act like they are the Emperor of the Earth and can do and say whatever the fuck they want, whenever they want and to whomever they want. Now, I can understand being a little conceited if you have some talent or skill, but most of the people you see with talent, are not so conceited when you meet them. It's the assholes who have dung between their ears, dung on their breath, can't read a soup label and can't afford to fill their gas tank who are the most snobbish. That is, the ones who can't back up being conceited because they are essentially worthless. Then there are the people who are conceited because of how other people are always telling them how great they are. These are the people with money, and the schmoozer's are building them up in order to tap in to that fortune.

- **Irresponsible**: People don't pay attention to anything. Especially if it's something that you need. You can't trust anybody to finish anything the right way if they are not being watched constantly. People are always seeking out a shortcut over a solution. If half the effort were put into quality that goes into looking for ways to cheat or do a slipshod job on something, all work would be damn near impeccable.

- **Ugly**: Wow we got ugly. What the fuck happened? Did we piss off whoever is in charge of the gene pool? The animal kingdom has restrictions on breeding. Even birds select the most attractive of their species, and there are some pretty ugly species of birds out there. You have to be either attractive or really strong and well built in order to earn mating rights where every creature on Earth is concerned, except for people. People will fuck anybody. So much for being the superior race on the planet.

- **Germaphobic**: People are scared of everything else, why not germs? Let's all be terrified of microscopic organisms we have no control over that we have lived with for millions of years. Let's invent soap that kills every bacterium except for the ones that actually harm us. Let's limit our exposure to bacteria so that our bodies can't build up proper immunities to them, and we get sick from shit that shouldn't bother us. Let's forget about the fact that many bacteria are symbiotic life forms that have adapted to human hosts, and that our bodies have accepted willingly. Let's forget that we actually need and use them for proper body regulation. Stupid people, micro-organisms are not your enemy, you are!

- **Selfish**: People are notoriously selfish. *"It's all about me and that is the bottom line"* should be the motto for the human race. I mean, there is nothing wrong with selfishness in general, it can be healthy. But like all things that are healthy, they are so in proper moderations. But people, like with all things they do, must do them in excess beyond what is reasonable, selfishness included. Humans have worked selfishness into an art form.

- **Suck-Ups**: People are schmoozer's, bottom line. If one person knows another person who has something more than they do and they think they can tap into that, *suddenly*, they are best friends. If someone runs into another person who is famous or well known, they want to be their best friend too. And why? Because they love them so much? Bullshit! It's because they want to see what they can get from that person. There is no admiration past the dollar signs that light up the eyes. When someone asks for an autograph do you think they are thinking, "gee, I met so-and-so"? Dead wrong, they are thinking, "gee, what's this worth"!

- **Wasteful**: People will throw away anything. If it's still good, if it still has use, if someone else can use it, fuck it, throw it away. People are great for insisting on too much of something and then not being able to use it. And rather than finding a use, they pitch it or burn it up. And then they lack the ability to learn a lesson in moderation. Can't handle the 64oz cup at the drive-thru and end up dumping it every time? Get a smaller cup next time? Fuck that, get a bigger cup next time! That's the human way!

- **Packrats**: When people aren't throwing away perfectly good shit, they are busy hoarding worthless shit. Who gives a shit about feeding the kids when you only have 25 out of 70 commemorative Civil War drinking glasses from the local gas station. And you will have to walk there to get them; you spent your gas money on the new "*Thumbprints of Executed Serial Killers*" stamp collection at the Post Office this morning…

- **Cowardly**: People are wimps. If there is an emergency they are always quick to find someone else to handle it for them. That is why there are so few true heroes. You are lucky to find one goat amongst ten thousand sheep. Everybody wants to huddle together or run. You hardly ever see the valiant independent that is willing to face the fear head on. Especially someone who does not expect praise or reward. No, the human animal is far too content with sniveling, yet they will cut down someone else for the same behavior. The human animal has become comfortable with cowering in the dark and shouting at their enemies back.

- **Conforming**: People are really good about fitting whatever mold will please the most people and keep them out of trouble. A rebel can be a pain in the ass, but sometimes a rebel can be a breath of fresh air. It is disturbing to me that so many people are comfortable with being something they are not in order to please someone whom they do not like or respect, because they are so worried about what these people might think. People are always willing to line right up, just like dominoes. Well, dominoes are knocked down pretty easily…

- **Imposing**: People are not just conformists. In fact, they are not happy unless everyone else is doing the same thing they are. That is how they help to self justify their behavior. "If I can convince, (or force) someone else to believe the same stupid shit that I do, then I must be right!" Or at least they can convince themselves that they are right for a short time. People are really well adapted when it comes to forcing other people into their same bullshit. And when you won't conform, then they attack your character like something is wrong with you for not joining the rest of the flock. So much for independence of thought.

- **Fanatically Religious**: I am going to say this one more time, religion and spirituality are not the same thing. Religion may be used by some to discover or achieve a form of spirituality that they are comfortable with, and that is fine. But religion in of itself is not spirituality as a whole, nor is any particular religion the only road toward a spiritual existence. People want to believe something, but they do not know what it is. So they follow along and, (here's that word again) <u>conform</u> to what others that present an air of authority offer up to them as truth. And deep in their subconscious they suspect that there is a possibility that it may not be the truth, so they seek to draw in the support of others. Numbers make people comfortable. *"If ten million people believe this, then there must be some truth to it"*, they tell themselves. These are the same people who become vicious when you are not interested in hearing about their version of a god. And here is the truth of this, if you believe something completely with no question or reservation in your mind, then when you encounter someone else who does not believe it, you are not challenged by that fact. <u>Them</u> not believing it is not a problem for <u>you</u>. But when you become angry that you are being challenged in your faith, you are actually challenging yourself because your faith is weaker than you thought. And as history has shown, this sort of self righteous angry fanaticism can be extremely dangerous.

- **Fearful**: People are afraid of anything that they do not know or understand. This is the main reason that so many people worldwide are so hypercritical of other cultures. If what others do is not the same as what is done where one person is, they criticize it and condemn it because they do not understand it. And this lack of understanding makes them afraid, a fear born of ignorance. It is an ignorance of self. And it makes people afraid of other people, animals, the dark, the ocean, and anything else you can think of from restaurant flatware to dust bunnies under the sofa. If it's unknown, even in the moment, people will be afraid of it. Fear is natural. And it wouldn't be so bad if people were not so ignorant as to learn about or face unknown factors instead of cowering from them or attacking them.

- **Unbalanced**: People cannot find the middle of anything. It is always one extreme or the other. Everything is hot or cold, black or white, there is never warm or grey. Even as was described above, in unknown factors the average person will cower or attack, there is hardly ever a middle ground with which to face off and get to know a situation and thus, get to know oneself.

A neutrality of thought by which a person can gather true perspective rather than making a snap judgment and assuming the premise of "*fight or flight*". How about "*be prepared and stay put*" so you can be balanced and at peace rather than fucking everything up all the time.

- **Lazy**: Oh my God people are lazy. Humans are masters of the shortcut and will half-ass anything they can to get out of work no matter how badly it needs to get done, even if it implies personal benefit. People want to lie around and let the world roll on without them, even if the world is rolling over them instead. Then they have the nerve to complain about the hardships they incur, even though most of the suffering is self imposed due to idleness. God, drag your asses away from the TV long enough to experience life, time runs out faster than you think.

- **Accusing**: People love to pass blame around. Scapegoats aplenty when trouble arises and no-one wants responsibility. Owning up to one's own liability is an almost unheard of practice. "*Yeah, I did that*." Is that so hard? When I admit things other people are shocked! They react that way because one, nobody admits anything, and two, they wouldn't admit anything, so why the hell am I? I must be stupid! Everyone seems to want to dump blame for a mistake or infraction on someone else if they can, they don't want to look bad. They would rather look stupid and bad because of their obvious dishonesty.

- **Daydreamers**: People's minds are always drifting off in la-la land rather than focusing on where they are and what they should be doing. People would rather fantasize about life instead of trying to live it. Then when they can't live up to the expectations of their fantasy, they look down on themselves for being less than what they expected. Too much time is spent standing around drooling while the world keeps turning.

- **Underachievers**: Saw this one coming, didn't you? People are always content with doing less than they are capable of. Even at the risk of never accomplishing anything of worth their entire lives. It starts in school. Public school expects very little from its students. Capable of A's, but B's will pass, hell, even a C will pass. But capable of an A, with a little more effort. But that will cut into TV time, right? Got a D or an F? No problem. A little modification of your grading standard will make that F and D into a C and B easily. So don't bother to do better, just hang by a thread your whole life why don't you?

- **Mean**: People are mean. They treat each other like shit. Then they have the nerve to complain about how they get treated by others, even though they do the same damn things. I will say it again, I have seen people treat their pets better than their friends, children, spouses, parents and relatives. And let's face it; most people are not all that nice to their pets either!

- **Depressed**: People are depressed. They feel like crap because of all the hardships in life. Unfortunately, there are two factors here that must be considered. First, most of the hardship is self imposed, we make it hard, we do it to ourselves. Second, life is hard anyway. Part of the problem is that people are unwilling to accept the fact that life is hard. They live under this illusion that other people have it easier, or that it is not so hard for them. Well, here's the big secret, it's hard for everybody. Even someone who is exceptionally wealthy can be suffering under the weight of their unhappiness and probably being jealous of you because your life seems simpler to them somehow. Quit whining about life and just live it.

- **Depressing**: Life is hard enough without everyone around you dragging you down because they are so busy feeling sorry for themselves. It's bad enough when I feel like crap, but then I have to listen to everyone else sniveling about how shitty their lives and health are. I have a headache, they have a migraine, I have a migraine, they have a concussion, I have a concussion, they have a skull fracture. Shut the fuck up! Not only is everyone depressed, they have to trump your depression. How dare I feel bad when someone else does? They have to convince me they feel worse somehow. Like I give a shit!

- **Lonely**: We are the most overpopulated creature on the planet next to the cockroaches, and we are so lonely. We are so afraid of each other and so afraid of ourselves that interpersonal communication has become a skill as rare as any other. And it's not only where strangers are concerned. I can understand not wanting to talk to someone you don't know. But we can't even talk to people we do know, and that's just sad. This is the reason that texting and chatting online have become so popular, it's safe. There is not really anybody there. You are staring at a screen and if you get scared, you can shut it off without fear of confrontation, with the other person or with your own conscience. Turn it off and tune it out, hide inside yourself and die frightened and alone. Is that how you want it?

- **Ignorant**: People don't seem to know anything, and they don't want to. They are uninformed or badly informed and naturally rude and arrogant about it. And sadly, people are comfortable with this. Rather than try and do and be better than what they are, they latch onto people who are better, and try to pull them down to their own level rather than attempt any small effort towards pulling themselves up, even a little.

- **Stupid**: This whole segment should be in all capital letters, because dear God people are stupid. They are not just stupid, they are fucking stupid! It's embarrassing how little common sense we demonstrate despite often having knowledge of exactly what is wrong with us and exactly what must be done to correct our problems. And not just personal problems, but problems involving the world around us. We are too busy wallowing in our own ignorance to stand up to our own selves and face who and what we really are so that we can improve and move forward. And that is just stupid…

Phrases That I Hate

Did you ever hear people say things that are just fucking stupid? But what they are saying are phrases that everyone else is saying, so it is extra annoying, especially if what they are saying is not exactly true. Often what is being said is being said because everyone else is saying it. People like to think that they are smart and that they are right. So if they hear something often enough, they will jump on the bandwagon to look intelligent or seem like they know what they are talking about, but they don't.

Well, if you are all finished being confused by what I am saying here, then read on and see some examples. Judge for yourself if I am crazy or not, (okay, so I'm crazy, but that doesn't mean that I can't be right).

The Children Are Our Future

If the children are our future, then we are all fucking doomed. We were a bunch of sniveling whining brats, and we raised the next generation to be just like us. Then because we didn't like them for being like us, we medicated them and altered their educational structure to over accommodate these whining brats up until they now hardly receive an education. We spend so much time so called helping them, that we end up hurting them instead.

Furthermore, to claim that they are the future is a copout. We don't want the responsibility of repairing the damage that we inherited that we couldn't deal with, and compounded with the additional mess that we added to it. So we say that someone else is the future, so they can get stuck with it, and we are supposed to somehow be proud of this?

Our children are burdened enough with existence itself without us not only dumping our problems on them, but making them feel like they are supposed to somehow take the reins and fix everything. Especially since we don't give them the nurturing or the tools that they need to succeed in regular life, never mind what we ask of them. Leave the children alone. Our parents didn't let us be children and didn't help us to grow up, and their parents didn't let them be children and didn't let them grow up and so on and so on. Break the cycle.

There Is No I In Team

Here is a phrase that you hear very often by people who want others to do things that they will not do themselves. Managers, bosses and supervisors are famous for it. It is meant to make you feel like your supposed independence is somehow a rebel non conformist attitude that will undermine the management and or the project. It is meant to make you feel that being different is somehow wrong, and that you should be a good worker bee. And as previously stated, the individuals saying this are rarely present when it's time to get the work done. So in other words, there may be no I in team, *but there is no U in it either.*

Things Are Getting Worse

Things are getting worse? Compared to when? This is a statement made by someone who never paid attention in history class. Written human history as far back as it records whether it be from an actual attempt to record an event, a story about an event, or some biblical account from whatever religion, records massive atrocities perpetrated by people against other people. People have always been mean, selfish, stupid and nasty. This has not changed one bit throughout history as we know it. Even the remains of bodies discovered from pre-history are often found brutalized or murdered. So what is new? The only difference between now and then is the volume of people. More people crammed into an overpopulated area are going to do more things, and certainly more bad things. If say, one out of every thousand people is a murderer, then in a town with a thousand people one nut is no big deal. But if you live in a city with a million people and the statistic stays the same, then it seems like more because of the higher volume of people. Additionally, this is compounded by media who sensationalize such events to promote their news, (which turns a profit based on advertising). Technology has changed, people have not. It is not any worse now than it ever was when you are talking about the human animal, as an animal.

Kids Are Getting Smarter

Compared to whom? Smarter than what? Are you kidding? Just because of vast and rapid advances in technology, you cannot say that kids are getting smarter. What we have here is a generation of button pushers who haven't the slightest idea how the equipment they are using works. Any moron can slide a mouse to their favorite porn website, that doesn't make them a fucking genius. It's the technology that seems smarter, not the people using it. And while we are all mesmerized by the sounds and flashing lights, each generation is losing valuable skills that have been eons in development. Natural selection of the species is supposed to be about the fittest and the smartest. But with the intervention of modern technology doing all the hard work for us, all we do is indiscriminately screw each other with no selection process outside of who can be the dirtiest in bed. We get fatter, lazier and stupider, while machines do all the work. Then because computers are making things easier, we want to pat ourselves on the back because our kids know how to operate a cell-phone or have a nineteen hour marathon with a video game that they think they are amazing for beating even though they used a book of cheats to win. And it's a book filled with symbol codes and pictures because they either don't have the patients to actually read it, or they simply can't fucking read anyway. You can't call a generation smarter for exchanging one skill set for another; especially when they are giving up <u>useful</u> skills for <u>useless</u> ones.

Computers Are Getting Smarter

Real simple, something incapable of independent thought cannot get smarter. Computers are getting easier to operate and more convenient, not smarter. Just because the average person is incapable of understanding exactly how a computer works does not mean that the computer is smarter, it means that the person operating the computer is dumber. And let us not forget that someone had to design, program and build the computer, they are the smart ones.

Failure Is Not An Option

Says who? Since when is failure not an option? Failure is absolutely an option and always has been. If failure were not an option then there would be disciplinary measures in place for people who are failures to either eliminate these people from the equation or help them progress into some degree of un-losers. There are not. What we do instead is modify their requirements so that they don't feel sorry for themselves for being failures, so that they won't bother the winners with their whining. I guess the assumption is that they are supposed to be so stupid that they don't know they are being tricked into having a false sense of self esteem. But the joke here is on the so called smart people, because the losers know they are failures, even though quite frankly many of them are stupid or at least underachievers. And when you try to pretend that they are not what you are really doing is patronizing them, and they can tell. So now not only are they supposed to be failures, but stupid as well. Not that any of them care, but it is better to be honest and say, "*you are stupid*", or "*you are a loser*" or if you want to be nice about it, "*you could do better, quit being an underachiever*" than to add an obvious lie to the problem making it ugly as well as foolish.

Turn That Frown Upside-down

Fuck you! I have a God given right to be miserable and pissed off if I damn please! As much as I gripe in this book, I certainly would not strip someone of their right to be upset about something. Who the hell am I? Certainly no better than anyone else. If someone is disturbed then let them work it out. Don't ask someone how the fuck they are if you don't want to hear the real answer. And I wish more people would tell the truth on this subject. *"How are you Frank?"* *"Oh, I'm good."* Bullshit, Frank is losing his fucking mind! But he tells the other guy what he wants to hear to shut him up because he doesn't want to tell him how he really feels because Frank knows the other guy doesn't really give a shit. So fuck him. Tell the truth. *"Oh, I feel like crap, didn't sleep at all last night, up with bad reflux and gas."* I bet you dude won't ask him again.

How's It Hanging

How's what hanging? Where? If it's what I think you are talking about then the answer is none of your fucking business! What the hell kind of question is this? How's it hanging? Who answers this, honestly? *"Hey Kevin, how's it hanging?"* *"Not too well actually, I'm wearing boxers and I seem to have slipped out the left side and stuck to my leg"*. Really people, can't we do better than this?

Have A Good One

Have a good what? Where? What is the one that I am supposed to have so good? I have heard this so many times that I am sure to have my *one* really amazingly as soon as I identify what the one is. What a stupid phrase.

Take A Piss

I have to take a piss, how many times have you heard that? I have to take a piss, take it where? From who? I thought the idea was that you were getting rid of it, not taking it from someone. Are you going into a restroom with a jar and looking for donations? Maybe you are just taking one with you somewhere. Walking around with a zipper bag full of urine for shits and giggles…

That's My Song

I hear this all the time, "*that's my song*". Is it? You wrote, choreographed, produced and performed it? Bullshit… You like the song, it is not <u>yours</u>. Get it straight! Another foul human trait, claiming things that people have no stake in. Grow up, saying this makes you sound like you are seven years old…

We're Not Promised Tomorrow

I hate this phrase. It is right up there with "*everybody dies*". It is an excuse, most often used by American youths as a way to justify not doing anything. People sit there and whine that they are not promised tomorrow, and do nothing today. Well, here is the truth in this statement. Tomorrow wasn't promised, and it is not promised, but tomorrow came and went, meanwhile you missed it pissing and moaning about something that may or may not be. You do not know what will happen in the next moment, tomorrow, next year or the next ten years but the reality is that you are likely to be here anyway because statistically the odds are massively against anything drastic ever actually happening to you. In the meantime, you are wasting your life and thereby wasting the lives of everyone around you by association. So quit making excuses for your sorry self and pull up your own goddamn bootstraps for once in your life. If something is going to take say four years, like a college degree, then guess what? You are going to very likely still be here in four years, whether or not you have either a degree or a lot of regret is up to you.

We're All In The Same Boat

We may all be in the same ocean, but we are defiantly not all in the same boat. Of if we are in the same boat, then I would have to point out that there is a considerable difference between general quarters and the VIP suites. This is said by people who want you to realize that their lives have problems too, even though they live in complete plush luxury and you eat dry supermarket brand cereal for every meal.

Time Heals All Wounds

Time may heal all wounds, but it still leaves plenty of scars. This phrase is meant well, but is often presented at the wrong time, and in the wrong way. When someone is wallowing in self pity because they just got dumped after a two year relationship they do not need the *time heals all wounds speech*. They need a pint of ice-cream and a shoulder to cry on. Shut up and give that person a hug and keep your feel good advice to yourself.

There's Plenty Of Other Fish In The Sea

This is up there with the *time heals all wounds* phrase. It is the epitome of the wrong thing said at the wrong time. Telling someone who has just been dumped yesterday that they will likely find someone else, is not helping the situation. Again, keep your bad advice to yourself, or at least present it differently. There may be plenty of fish in the sea, but that only matters if you don't care what you catch or how.

Your Vote Counts

While numerically speaking this may be true, whether or not it actually counts is open for debate. The government likes to get large voter participation because it adds weight to their statistics that show how involved everyone is, adding clout to their particular party as it is empowered. But in situations like with the Electoral College for example, your vote isn't worth the hole you punched out. First of all, who picks the candidates? You? No, they do. Often, as with the presidency, the parties already have everyone they are willing to tolerate lined up before the voting even starts, you just sort them out. Then when the candidates are narrowed down, it is time for the Electoral College to decide who actually wins the bid, and this is usually determined by how many of the Electoral voters are of the same party ticket as the candidate, and has little or even nothing to do with skills or ability, (a lesson you should have all learned when Bush won his second bid). Then you end up with a bonehead who's only qualification was that he picked correctly when he was given the choice between declaring himself either Democrat or Republican, because God knows that no-one else from any party has a chance in hell of getting that far in America anymore.

The Electoral College was a failsafe mechanism put in place by the founding fathers because they thought that the average voter was too stupid and ignorant to be trusted with such an important decision. The downside of this last statement is that for many, it rings true.

Equality

I hate this word. It is necessary for some, but for too many it is an excuse. And to them I say this; there is no such thing as equality. There is no-one on earth that is truly equal with anyone else. We are all different. If we were all the same, then we would be equal, and we would be boring. Squirrels are equal. They all look the same, act the same, and do the same things the exact same way. Jellyfish are equal. Do you want to be a jellyfish? Equality is boring. Aside from an opposable thumb our differences are the only other thing that truly sets us apart from the animals. It is our greatest strength and weakness at the same time. But good or bad it keeps us interesting. So who really wants to be equal? Everyone who cries for equality does not want to be equal. Everyone wants to be *superior*, not equal. People who strive for excellence do not ask for equality, because they have a <u>superiority</u> about them. They are athletic or scholarly or can sing really well or play an instrument really well or draw or something like that. Equality is the battle cry of the underachiever. The low man who has no self esteem or ambition calls for equality because they feel inferior, but lack the willpower to push themselves to a higher level. Equality gives them the opportunity to pull the rest of the world down to their level so that they do not have to achieve anything.

Fair

Fair is another word I hate. Fair is the mantra of the losers. You know who you are! Winners do not complain about what is fair. That is because they are too busy being the best they can at what they do. I'm talking about true losers mind you, not the ones who came in second or third, or even the last person across the line in a marathon, I'm talking about the ones who didn't even enter the race. These are the same types as the people who want equality. They have no initiative, they are lazy, and they do not even want to try because they have defeated themselves before they even started. But they feel the sting of not getting noticed, so they cry about what is fair. You want fair? Then fucking try, really try! Don't do it once and quit because it's hard, that's what losers do. Stop being a loser; it's a burden on everybody else. Losers always quit, or they don't even start.

God Is Going To Find Me A Man

Women, I hate to single you out here, but there is a phrase that I have heard once too often from women, (Christian women in particular) that applies here. And that phrase is "*God is going to find me a man*". Is He? Really? Listen, even if God found you a man, he is not going to knock on your door with a man and a certified letter explaining that this is your new man. Get out there and look. Because what you really mean to say, is that the last guy hurt you so bad, either physically or emotionally, that you have become afraid to look. Waiting on an unanswered prayer is your excuse for not looking, or even trying. Quit waiting for someone else to handle your problems for you, God or otherwise. If you are lonely, do something about it.

My God!

Okay, even I'm guilty of this one. Saying my God is engrained into language like cussing is. You say it without even realizing it because everyone says it, even atheists say it. It's habitual language. But let us think about this for a moment. Whose God? This is an example of the thought or idea of God or a god like entity being used in the possessive. Suffice it to say that just about any religion you can find implies that we belong to God, not the other way around. To claim God as a possession is to demean the concept. The correct way to exclaim this would be to say something like "*the God of me*", I know, it sounds lame, but it would be truer to the point. But giving God a possessive gives humans the imaginary power to claim God in thought and deed, reducing any God if such exists to the level of imaginary friend. "*I don't hate you, God does*". *I don't want to hurt you, God wants me to*".

Other ways to twist this around and make God more convenient are with terms people use to metaphorically describe God. For example, people use phrases with and say words like *lord, king, father, prince, master* and many other phrases like them. All of these words are *humanizing* words. They are words that lower the standard of an entity such as a god or God because of the human intellects inability to properly comprehend such a creature. To call God even a king is to lower God's stature to a human level, thus creating the imaginary subconscious line akin to some sort of equality with such a being. This is a preposterous suggestion when comparing a human being to an entity who is supposed to be capable of spontaneously creating life with pure thought alone. Only a human could have such presumptuousness, such arrogance.

The Big Lie

Make no mistake, people lie. But even worse, those being lied to eat it up. People love the lie. They don't want to know the real truth about anything. People prefer to live in a perpetual illusion either self created or absorbed from an outside source. Anything to keep from facing themselves or facing reality. They want to be lied to, people simply adore it. And as it is so loved, there are many that are equally willing to accommodate the lies being told for their own fun and profit.

Many of these in particular are perpetrated by politicians, religious leaders, community leaders, and others who know that the average individual really has no idea what the hell is being told to them anyway. But if people are being told something that they think will benefit them, even if it won't, and even if they know it won't, they want to believe it anyway and that is enough. A smart person knows how to manipulate this.

In other words, if you are willing to take it, someone is willing to dish it out. So open wide, here it comes…

Minimum Wage

Minimum wage is the lowest amount it is legal to pay someone unless they are wait-staff and are expected to supplement their income with gratuities. Now obviously people do not want to work for minimum wage because they hardly make any money to live off of. I have been there, having to pull down two jobs to pay the rent, it sucks. Now the illusion here is, (and politicians love this one) that if you raise the minimum wage it will improve the lives of people hanging in the balance of the poverty scale. This is a big lie, and here's why.

1. If you are taking home like $200 a week after taxes raising the minimum wage a few cents or a dollar is not going to make any difference in the quality of life for people in this situation.

2. Most people working in these jobs are working them for a reason. They either do not have the intelligence, education, physical capacity or willpower for anything else, or they have an addiction of some kind or are in a situation that does not allow for them to be recognized by better jobs like being located in an area with a slumping job market or they have felonies for example.

3. If the minimum wage was drastically increased, the companies that pay these sorts of wages would raise the prices on their goods and services to cover the difference of loss because payroll is almost always the largest expense of any company and therefore the employer's bottom line.

4. It is for this reason also that more people would lose their jobs, and the people who are still working would be forced to multitask at an even higher rate in order to keep their lousy jobs.
5. Minimum wage is minimum wage for a reason. A company very often gets what they pay for. There are many good workers stuck in the minimum wage bracket, but there are just as many who are often enough either derelicts who can't work anywhere else or foreigners who appreciate any job instead of being stuck up about it because of the conditions they have come from in their own country.

    It is hard for me to listen to people whine about low wages when I have had to live off of collecting bottles and cans out of garbage to feed my kids in the past. It is equally as annoying for me to have had high paying jobs later in life and have to listen to slobbering fools complain about their jobs as well while pulling down three to five time minimum with full benefits.

Parenting

Giving birth does not a parent make. Not everyone is cut out to be a parent, and many shouldn't even try. And let's face it, most pregnancies are accidents. It is a minority situation that a child is deliberately planned for and conceived. Granted that many people are perfectly happy about this accident when it does happen, and goes along with it and all is well, but this is rare. But for the majority where it is unwanted and unexpected, they need to own up to that.

Now, I'm not suggesting running out and getting an abortion. That is not what I am driving at. I am talking about full term pregnancies that result in actual births here. My beef is with people who have the baby, and keep it when they shouldn't.

I'm talking about people who have a baby that they don't know what to do with and don't want it, and yes, even actually resent it, but keep the child. Listen, if you have a baby and don't want it, somebody does. Give it away before it is too late and you end up with an unloved unwanted teenage delinquent who will ultimately become you when they grow up and fuck up a child of their own by repeating the mistake that you made. All you will do is raise this little person with scorn, neglect and abuse. And don't think they will not understand that they are not loved, liked or wanted. Little people may not be able to think logically, but they can feel.

The problem is that society expects parents to do the right thing, and with everyone watching, parents will pretend that they care to save face or avoid embarrassment. They are more concerned with looking like they care than facing the truth and saying, "*I can't do this*", or even more realistically, "*I don't want to do this*". I would rather see people be honest about it no matter how people look at them. If it drags out too long, the child will end up in state custody as a teenager when they are too old for anyone to want and too full of neuroses to ever have a normal life. Do the right thing, face the truth and let go. There are plenty of people here that would love to adopt your child. Other countries practically sell their unwanted children to Americans, and this goes on because adoption is so amazingly difficult here.

Leadership

I am sick and tired of hearing how we are raising a nation of leaders. Where are they? We are raising a nation of followers, with no leaders in sight. Anyone proclaiming to be a leader is more along the lines of a manipulator who is only occupied with their own selfish interests. Independent thought is being bred out of our youth. And even if everyone was made into a leader, then there would be no followers, and that would be even worse.

Let's face it; no-body is leading anyone anywhere unless there is a buck to be made in it somehow.

Gun Control

Oh, I love this one. Gun control. Let's all pretend that the world would be a safer and better place if there were no guns. Interesting notion. Only one problem with it, the people would still be here. And if they don't have a gun, guess what? They will find another way. People have been viciously and selfishly slaughtering one another over bullshit since before recorded history; it isn't going to change because you restrict a particular type of weapon. And please don't insult me by giving me shooting statistics from countries that are much smaller than America that have staggering numbers of deaths by stabbings and beatings, or by telling me about a larger country with better crime control if that country uses extreme brutality to enforce their laws.

And furthermore don't insult me with crime statistics. What you are often not told about robberies and shootings is that many of these guns are stolen. No person who goes through all the trouble, training and expense it takes to get a legal registered firearm and license is going to blow the whole thing by holding up a convenience store for $52.

And yes, if you take away people's legal right to own a firearm then you are setting them up to be victims. Because a criminal who is determined will find a way, illegally, that is what makes them criminals. People only obey the law if they want to.

A gun is a tool, same as a hammer. And if the gun is not available, be prepared to have your head nailed to something.

Overcrowded Prisons

Here is another statistic that politicians love to manipulate. The overcrowded prison system in America. You hear it all the time how we have more people in prison than any other country including those countries that are larger than us. This is for the most part true. But why do you think this is? The <u>why</u> is the part you never hear, because it implies weakness on our part, and it reveals the ignorance of the people who believe anything told to them by the media without investigating it for themselves.

There are several non American alternatives in the rest of the world when it comes to managing criminal activity. Here is a short list of contrasts to give you an idea.

1. The country does not have the same laws that we do on account of their culture and so things that are illegal here are not illegal elsewhere.
2. The country is broke and has a bare bones police force if they have a police force at all,

and therefore is helpless to uphold their system of law.

3. The country has a criminal force that is better funded and more organized than their government, and pretty much does what it pleases.

4. The country is so staggeringly strict that everyone is terrified to commit a crime.

5. Rehabilitation is actually a form of government sanctioned slavery.

6. The prison facilities themselves look like something from 15th century Europe and are run by the modern equivalent of the Spanish Inquisition.

7. Executions are particularly brutal, and torture is a standard procedure.

8. Anyone who does commit even a minor crime is executed or given a jail sentence so long that death is a better alternative.

You hear this last one particularly often from politicians with the example of comparing the United States to Russia and China. They like to tell us that we have more prisoners than Russia and China combined. Here's the part they don't tell you. If you are arrested in Russia you would be lucky to make it to jail in the first place. They are not currently practicing the death penalty, but any Russian will tell you that one in five people arrested are practically beaten to death anyway, (A minor throwback from the Uncle Joe's Communist USSR way of handling crime). I wouldn't want to commit a crime there either. And you remember China, with their mobile execution vans? They need them; they have the highest execution ratio in the world. In 2005 for example, if I remember correctly the US executed 60 people, however in the same year, China reported around 10,000, (that they admit to). Think about it…

The End Of An Empire

There is a lot of speculation about the end of the United States of America as we know it. When and how it will happen, and most importantly, why, is ripe for speculation. America is often compared to the old Roman Empire, an empire that got too big for its britches so to speak, and lost its way. An empire that fell apart, as many think America will, because of its decadence and weak management. Perhaps so. But I don't think that was the problem, and even though America has too much decadence and weak management, it is not ultimately the problem. So what is the problem?

The real problem is already here, and it is not coming from the federal government, at least not directly. The real problem is coming from state and local governments, and it is a problem being overlooked by federal regulation because it considers such things to be the individual states problems. And what is the problem?

The problem is that the state and local governments of every state in the union is in everyone's fucking business. They want to tell all of their citizens what to do and how to do it all the time and won't leave them alone. And in particular, they attack the middle class. They attack the middle class because they think this will set an example, because the majority of population is lower class or poverty or below, and it seems like they are picked on anyway and the state wants it to look like they are not profiling. They accomplish this by profiling the middle class and upper class income earners instead. This is a smokescreen.

What is not being realized is that they are targeting the people who are voters, decision makers, workers and skilled laborers, and from the state's perspective, the biggest taxpayers by volume. There is only so much disruption that anyone can take from authority, particularly authority that proclaims your freedom at every opportunity while they slowly take it away.

Sooner or later one family too many is going to have its children taken away because they took a picture of their kid playing on the beach, or get one more threatening letter from the District Attorney's office because their kid missed a day of school, and the whole structure is going to come crumbling down. These people will band together and fight, and the local government won't be able to handle it, they are simply not equipped for such a thing. Then the feds will step in and muddle the whole thing up because they will not truly understand the problem. All they will do is throw money at it, like they do with every other problem. That is how America fails its people, and that is what will cause America to fall.

Not because of terrorism, not because of economics, or war, and not because of poor health and eating habits. But because the individual states use social services to police, intimidate and basically strong-arm its citizens with the threat of losing their children.

In Closing

Listen; let me sum up all of this complaining into a simple statement. There is the person that you are, the person that you think you are, the person that you want everyone else to see, and the person that you ought to be. So, which is the right person? Really, the obvious answer would be the person that you ought to be. But that requires a great deal of virtue, and it is very hard to achieve. And even the truly virtuous person realizes that they still may not be right, at least not in every instance. Perfection is not possible, make no mistake about this. But also realize that one must strive for perfection, even while realizing that they will likely never achieve it, or even come close. You could just be who you are, and that is fine. Provided you really know who you are, and few people really do. This leaves most people trapped in one of the middle categories. That is, who you think you are, which is a lie you tell to yourself, and who you want everyone else to see, which is a lie to yourself and to others. This lie is much worse. But any lie told to the self is ultimately very destructive. In the meantime, try finding a symmetry balancing yourself between all of these versions of self. If you are true to yourself in this endeavor, then eventually, you may gravitate to either the person you are, or the person you ought to be. But I make no promises...

There, now don't I feel better having gotten all of that off of my chest, and aren't you relieved that I have stopped. I can go back to pretending to be nice now. Yeah, right...